SAMUEL BECKETT
PLAYWRIGHT & POET

SAMUEL BECKETT
PLAYWRIGHT & POET

EDITED BY CHRISTOPHER MURRAY

PEGASUS BOOKS
NEW YORK

SAMUEL BECKETT
PLAYWRIGHT & POET

Pegasus Books LLC
80 Broad Street
5th Floor
New York, NY 10004

First Pegasus Books edition 2009

Library of Congress Cataloging-in-Publication Data is available.

ISBN: 978-1-60598-002-7

10 9 8 7 6 5 4 3 2 1

Printed in the United States of America
Distributed by W. W. Norton & Company, Inc.
www.pegasusbooks.us

CONTENTS

acknowledgments

A cknowledgments are due Louis le Brocquy and Pierre le Brocquy for permission to reproduce the image of Beckett on the cover. We also thank Declan Cantwell, Director of Finance and Administration, the Abbey Theatre, for permission to reproduce photographs from productions of Beckett's plays staged at the Abbey and the Peacock together with details from some programmes, and archivist Mairéad Delaney for much-appreciated help. Also Marie Rooney, Deputy Director, the Gate Theatre, for permission to use images from Gate productions, and to Jenni Rope for her consideration at a busy time at the Gate. We thank Dr Raymond Refausée and the Representative Church Body Library for permission to publish Beckett's baptismal record. Thanks also to Theo Dorgan and Poetry Ireland for help with the image from *The Great Book of Ireland/ Leabhar Mór na hÉireann.*

list of illustrations

1 Beckett's baptismal certificate, with date of birth recorded, Register, Tullow Church (courtesy Church of Ireland Representative Church Body Library).

2 Cover of *Eleutheria*, first published in 1995 by Éditions de Minuit, Paris.

3 Peter O'Toole, Eamon Kelly and Donal McCann in *Waiting for Godot*, directed by Sean Cotter, Abbey Theatre, 1969 (courtesy Abbey Theatre).

4 Programme for Irish translation of *Godot* made by Liam Ó Briain and Sean Ó Carra, directed by Alan Simpson for An Taibhdhearc, 1971 (private collection).

5 Programme for *Film* and *Play*, directed by Eddie Golden, Peacock, 1967 (courtesy Abbey Theatre).

6 Marie Kean in *Happy Days*, directed by Jim Sheridan, Peacock, 1973 (courtesy Abbey Theatre).

7 Programme for *That Time*, Peacock, 1978 (courtesy Abbey Theatre).

8 John Hurt in *Krapp's Last Tape*, directed by Robin Lefèvre, Gate Theatre, 1991 (courtesy Gate Theatre).

9 Susan Fitzgerald as May in *Footfalls*, directed by Derek Chapman, Gate Theatre, 1991 (courtesy Gate Theatre).

10 Godfrey Quigley and Barry McGovern in *Endgame*, directed by Ben Barnes, Peacock, 1984 (photograph: Fergus Bourke).

11 and 12 Programme for *I'll Go On*, 1985, a one-man show featuring Barry McGovern, adapted from Beckett's trilogy by Barry McGovern and Gerry Dukes (courtesy Gate Theatre).

13 Poster/Programme for the San Quentin Drama Workshop production of *Krapp's Last Tape* and *Endgame*, [as] directed by Beckett, 1980 (private collection).

14 Flo McSweeney as Hands in Nacht und Träume, directed by Sarah-Jane Scaife, Peacock, 1990 (courtesy Abbey Theatre).

15 Beckett's manuscript entry, 'Da Tagte Es', from *The Great Book of Ireland/ Leabhar Mór na hÉireann*, 1989 (by permission of the Trustees).

I t is interesting to note that the centenary of Beckett's birth takes place on the centenary of Ibsen's death. It means that 1906 was a major turning point in the history of theatre and drama. The writers were poles apart in the truest sense. Ibsen, as the eighteen-year-old Joyce was quick to see, was the greatest exponent of dramatic realism of his day, a fearless analyst of middle-class lives in all their cosy hypocrisies. Beckett, in contrast, held realism in contempt and when he found his own artistic voice, as distinct from an echo of Joyce's, it was to sing of human solitude and suffering in a world at once risible and profoundly tragic. Neatly, symmetrically half-way through the twentieth century in 1953, Beckett hit upon a play which was to speak to all peoples and all nations of human anxiety and endurance in the face of a godless universe. *Waiting for Godot* was his *A Doll's House*, even though it is not on record that the latter was ever described as the laugh sensation of two continents. Beckett changed the terms by which we begin to understand our troubled identity. His career as a whole, as poet, writer of fiction and plays in many styles and modes, redefined our world for us, shaming us into recognising ourselves in the shocking, Christ-like images he presented of the incarcerated, the mentally disturbed, the lonely, all those at the end of their tether. His, like Ibsen's, was a fearless journey across difficult terrain towards whatever ease and warmth are released by holding the course. If Ibsen knew the Ice Church (*Brand*) and the 'icy metal hand that clutches the heart' and kills (*John Gabriel Borkman*), Beckett knew the hellish blazing light that tortures (*Happy Days*) and the more than handfuls of dust, 'from floor to ceiling nothing only dust', which overwhelm like the void 'pouring in on top of you' (*That Time*). But Beckett knew laughter too and wore his rue with a difference. He had the courage of his convulsions.

And so we remember and honour Samuel Beckett on his hundredth birthday as a supreme artist and master builder. He is now among the greats. But like all great writers he created the taste by which he is to be understood. It is very much the purpose of this collection of Thomas Davis lectures to explore this taste, so to enquire into Beckett's matchless skills as shaper and inventor as to provide firm Hibernian ground for the appreciation and understanding of his work and thought. Providing ground on air was not the least of the challenges posed by this project. It is entirely to the credit of the contributors that they faced the challenges as Beckett might have wished, stoically and with good humour, and produced fine work in saluting fine work. As editor, I am proud of what they have done. Through their efforts Beckett's manifold imagination comes to life once again in the pages of a book, so that it is no longer a matter of contemplating the awful prospect of 'Imagination Dead Imagine' but rather of celebrating his wonderful 'Imagination Live Imagine' now and let us hope for times to come.

Seamus Hosey of RTÉ has been enormously supportive from the inception of this Thomas Davis series, and his advice and organisational skills have been invaluable. Deirdre Nolan, editor at New Island, has likewise given constant support. They have been two extra contributors to this project and I thank them both sincerely.

Christopher Murray

CHRISTOPHER MURRAY

introduction: panting on to a hundred

In Beckett's first and best radio play, *All That Fall*, there is this delicious speech uttered by a typically ill-tempered husband to his put-upon wife who has made the mistake of asking him on his birthday if he is not well: 'Well! Did you ever know me to be well? The day you met me I should have been in bed. The day you proposed to me the doctors gave me up. You knew that, did you not? The night you married me they came for me with an ambulance. You have not forgotten that I suppose?' The series of reversals of the usual point of view in marital relationships, 'the day *you* proposed to me' and 'the night *you* married me', comically indicate Beckett's topsy-turvy world well enough, but so too do the sentences which follow if we bear in mind that the speaker, Dan Rooney, though still gainfully employed – just about – is four score years and upward: 'No, I cannot be said to be well. But I am no worse. Indeed I am better than I was. The loss of my sight was a great fillip. If I could go deaf and dumb I think I might pant on to be a hundred. Or have I done so? [*Pause.*] Was I a hundred today? [*Pause.*] Am I a hundred, Maddy?'[1] This wonderful barrage is greeted with silence. The Beckett style, as humorous as it is bleak, is here beautifully inscribed on air. Beckett himself was to die at roughly the same age Dan Rooney achieved in this radio play. Had he panted on to a hundred he might be addressing you here this evening instead of your humble servant, though I wouldn't put money on it. It could have been twenty-nine minutes of silence.

At any rate, here we are on the hundredth birthday of Samuel Barclay Beckett, a cause for celebration even if he, like most of the characters he created, saw little to celebrate in such matters. 'Birth was the death of him,' he allowed one of his later monologuists to intone.[2] A few years back Christopher Ricks wrote a witty book under the unpromising title *Beckett's Dying Words*, the point of which was to illustrate how astringent the pessimism can be. Patrick Kavanagh, surprisingly, had made a similar point in a review of the text of *Waiting for Godot* in 1956. 'All of us who are sincere,' said Kavanagh, 'know that if we are unhappy, trying to forget our futility in pubs, it is due to no exterior cause, but to what is now popularly called the human condition.' Kavanagh was astute in observing that to deny the misery, for whatever reason, was to be dishonest. 'It is because of its awareness of the peculiar sickness of society and a possible remedy suggested,' he went on, 'that I like Beckett's play.'[3] We can come back to this question of a remedy later on. For now let us, like true Beckettians, stay with the misery.

He himself told the story of the English intellectual who grilled him at a party as to why he always wrote about distress and who thought him perverse when Beckett conceded he had had a happy childhood and his mother had not run away from home. 'I left the party as soon as possible and got into a taxi. On the glass partition between me and the driver were three signs: one asked for help for the blind, another for orphans, and the third for relief for the war refugees.' He concluded: 'One does not have to look for distress. It is screaming at you even in the taxis of London.'[4] It is commonplace to observe that at bottom Beckett saw all this suffering as absurd. That is no doubt the case, but it would be quite wrong to see this attitude as in any way complacent or (worse) in Byron's adolescent vein when he quipped, 'And if I laugh at any mortal thing,/'Tis that I may not weep.' Beckett's sense of the absurd was tragic and imbued with compassion; it did not dress escapism in any other garb but black. Thus we have the laughably lugubrious certainties of Watt in the novel of the same name, as Watt reflects upon the so-called wonders of the natural world in its eternal cycles, life itself, and arrives at these sentences, not to say conclusion:

> And if I could begin it all over again knowing what I know now, the result would be the same. And if I could begin again a third time, knowing what I would know then, the result would be the same. And if I could begin it all over again a hundred times, knowing each time a little more than the time before, the result would always be the same, and the hundredth life as the first, and the hundred lives as one. [...] But at this rate we shall be here all night.[5]

Watt was written in France during the darkest days of World War Two and yet remains consistently a funny book. I think the scholars may allow me to say that all of Beckett's leading figures, for one dare not call them heroes, aim for Nirvana and miss. Like the first of these figures in the fiction, Murphy, or the first in the plays, Victor in *Eleutheria*, they try to obliterate the self, nothing being so painful as consciousness to an awakened sensibility, only to find themselves going in circles. If we care to, we might see Schopenhauer's *The World as Will and Idea* behind much of this series of vain attempts by Beckett's characters to outwit the way things are. But time enough for that exercise, perhaps, when we have heard later on in this series from another speaker on Beckett and philosophy. Our task is to try to see how comedy and tragedy combine in his work.

We're beginning to find here that to introduce or reintroduce Beckett in his centenary year is also to sum up. We have glanced at his tragicomic emphasis, his angle of vision. But we need to see how original this vision was and how controlled and courageous. The idea of the inadequacy of tragedy for the twentieth century was probably first introduced by Chekhov, who showed how comedy is often better suited to plumb the depths of despair. In his own way, Seán O'Casey developed an Irish version of tragicomedy, starting with *The Shadow of a Gunman* in 1923, continuing through *Juno and the Paycock* in 1924 and culminating in his masterpiece *The Plough and the Stars* in 1926. Beckett saw these first productions at the Abbey. He came to admire how O'Casey used 'the principle of knockabout' [farce] at the domestic level to dramatise collapse, 'mind and world come asunder in irreparable dissociation – "chassis"', at the social and political levels.[6] The drama after 1945 tended to endorse this tragicomic mode. But Beckett took the idea to extremes O'Casey could not accept. O'Casey's main objection serves to show how drama was now taking two main forms, the politically conscious and the studiously non-political. It angered O'Casey that Beckett seemed to be saying, to quote the opening line of *Waiting for Godot*, that there was 'nothing to be done'. That he could not accept. For him change was always a possibility; indeed, if justice was to be achieved, a necessity. Thus, O'Casey wrote, 'his [Beckett's] philosophy isn't my philosophy, for within him there is no hazard of hope, no desire for it; nothing in it but a lust for despair, and a crying of woe.'[7] Beckett's route was to be independent of the Irish one, and independent too of much of the European dramatic tradition from Ibsen on. Arthur Miller, for example, took a stand on behalf of a drama, a form of tragedy rather than of tragicomedy, which deliberately opposed the theatre of the absurd which Beckett helped create. Writing in the introduction to the first volume of his *Collected Plays* in 1958, Arthur Miller declared: 'The assumption – or presumption – behind these plays [such as *All My Sons*, *Death of a Salesman* and *The Crucible*] is that life has meaning.' A lot of other playwrights agreed. Beckett bravely dissented.

Miller pointed out that the purpose of drama is 'the creation of a higher consciousness and not merely a subjective attack upon the audience's nerves and feelings.'[8] Beckett might have agreed that the task was to put modern consciousness on the stage, or in the novel for that matter, but he would surely have balked at calling it 'a higher consciousness'. The consciousness Beckett was interested in was of the abyss. There is the passage in *Endgame* (1958) where Hamm wonders if he and Clov aren't beginning to 'mean something', which Clov scoffingly rejects and Hamm defends: 'Imagine if a rational being came back to earth, wouldn't he be liable to get ideas into his head if he observed us long enough. [*Voice of rational being.*] Ah, good, now I see what it is, yes, now I understand what they're at!' But the passage ends up laughably with Hamm grasping at straws: 'And without going so far as that, we ourselves … [*with emotion*] … we ourselves … at certain moments … [*Vehemently.*] To think it won't all have been for nothing!' (*CDW* 108) Clov meantime cries out in anguish that he has a flea on his person. A whole philosophical debate is reduced to a fleabite. Not much chance of changing the situation here, or indeed in any of the surreal situations Beckett puts on stage as images of human experience. In such situations consciousness is in flight from horror. Hamm and Clov dwell in a world in free fall towards annihilation.

In his little book on Proust, published as early as 1931 and still essential reading for anyone who wants to understand Beckett himself, he said we are faced with either living a life of thoughtless 'habit' or with accepting the stark reality of 'the suffering of being'. It is Hobson's choice for the intelligent person. As Beckett repeatedly illustrates through his habit-bound characters, the self-deception of human kind, male and female, is incorrigible. As he puts it: 'The pendulum oscillates between these two terms: Suffering – that opens a window on the real and is the main condition of the artistic experience, and Boredom […] that must be considered as the most tolerable because the most durable of human evils.'[9] I am bored therefore I am. But I am bored because I won't face up to the reality, which is that the world is one of two things, a hospital (mental, for preference) or a top-security prison, from neither of which is release possible. It's like Mephostophilis' reply to Faustus, who wonders how he can wander about the earth at liberty: 'Why, this is hell, nor am I out of it.'[10] For Beckett the truth is here, in the despair. And from this point he can move on, at least in the imagination. It was a journey equal to Dante's in the middle of that dark wood. Only for Beckett the journey was also in some measure comic, taking it for granted that, as he says in *Endgame*, 'nothing is funnier than unhappiness [...] it's the most comical thing in the world' (*CDW* 101).

It is because Beckett believed that to be is to suffer and that at the same time pain is evil that he saw life itself as fundamentally evil. I think by this he meant the terms on which life is offered, its brevity, its loneliness, the fragility of love and so on. It is what we cannot usually avoid, even if we should choose to live as reclusively as some of Beckett's solitary figures, like Joe in the television play *Eh Joe* (1966), who is afraid to go to bed at night even though he has checked every nook and corner of his room for hidden terrors. A woman's voice speaks to him as he sits uneasily on the edge of his bed at night:

Thought of everything? ... Forgotten nothing? ... You're all right now, eh? ... No one can see you now ... No one can get at you now ... Why don't you put out that light? There might be a louse watching you ...Why don't you go to bed? ... What's wrong with that bed, Joe? (*CDW* 362)

The voice torments him with memories of past relationships, in particular with a lover whom he turned off and who committed suicide. In slow accumulation of detail the voice describes the scene where the woman combined pills with drowning on Killiney beach in the nighttime. 'Imagine what in her mind to make her do that ... Imagine ... Trailing her feet in the water like a child. ... Takes a few more [pills] on the way ... Will I go on, Joe? ... Eh Joe?' The voice is relentless. 'There's love for you ... Eh Joe?' (*CDW* 366). I think this play marks an unusual disclosure by Beckett that he was a deep-dyed humanist. He was no Dadaist, no believer in the superficial hand of chance. He accepted responsibility and demanded that his characters did likewise. The voice within, the consciousness which will not let Joe rest, is really conscience in disguise, the notion of *numquam minus solus quam solus*, never less alone than when we are alone. It is a common burden for Beckett's characters to bear, which is why they create the company of other voices to console and assuage. In another century Beckett would have been talking about original sin. Instead, what he actually says is, 'the tragic figure represents the expiation of original sin [...] the sin of having been born.'[11] This is the source of the inescapable guilt present throughout Beckett's work. Unlike the work of Arthur Miller or any other writer of social drama this guilt is never resolved through action, by means of a plot. It is a persistent condition, to be dissolved only in death, which Beckett happily supplies in his last plays, especially in *That Time*, where no less than three inner voices or memories haunt the last moments of the central character called the Listener.

This deeply Protestant, not to say Puritanical, obsession with the guilt of being allowed Beckett to create a body of plays which are deeply tragic in theme and expression. They present us with what in classical drama and in Shakespeare would be termed catastrophe and catharsis, the purgation to be experienced by seeing the representation of human suffering in the extreme. Instead of a full tragedy, Beckett's plays give us only act five every time. And it is because we never, through plot development, see the *cause* of the suffering that his work sharply differs from the conventional form of tragedy where the catastrophe is traceable to a root in some error by or moral flaw in the hero. Lack of a cause would not do O'Casey, for whom a socialist analysis could provide the reason for human suffering. Lack of a cause would not do for Miller, for whom a psychological analysis could reveal the roots of the aberrant behaviour leading to catastrophe. James Joyce argued that in tragedy the spectator is not only united with the sufferer in pity but also united with what he called 'the secret cause', undefined and indefinable.[12] In Beckett's work the secret cause dominates all.

But of course this is only half of what Beckett does. As we know, the impression a Beckett play creates in the playing, though not in the overall effect, is of hilarious comedy. We call it comedy of the absurd or comedy of despair but it is a positive thing in any case, an expenditure of vital energy and high spirits in the face of the oncoming darkness. It is not just whistling past the graveyard; it is gaining entry with variety entertainers, at least in the early work. Indeed, graveyards and Beckett seem to go hand in hand. As one of his narrators breezily remarks, 'Personally I have no bone to pick with graveyards, I take the air there willingly, perhaps more willingly there than elsewhere, when take the air I must.'[13] No other author manages to derive such humour from death and its encumbrances. The narrator aforesaid of 'First Love' amuses himself in the graveyard where his father's remains contribute to the atmosphere and where the narrator is inspired to compose his own epitaph:

Hereunder lies the above who up below
So hourly died that he lived on till now.

Even suicide is sometimes introduced as a subject of mirth, as more than once in *Waiting for Godot*, to stray no further.

But I want now to take a look at a much less well-known play, Beckett's first, written in French in 1947, never staged and not even translated until after Beckett's death. Perhaps it is no more than the scrapings of the Beckettian barrel, then, but yet it is a piece which is challenging in many ways and one which deserves to be better known. It is called *Eleutheria*, meaning 'freedom'. Here the young anti-hero, ironically called Victor Krap, is a total deadbeat, a drop-out before the term was coined, and a hopeless depressive. Apart from all that he is an interesting character. In some respects this play is surprisingly conventional, being a three-act study of a middle-class family and its troublesome son. In other respects it is quite radical and reminiscent of Albert Camus. It also introduces on stage a spectator who complains about the boring proceedings and the poor writing: 'Actually, who wrote this rubbish? [*he consults programme*] Beckett [*he says "Béké"*], Samuel, Béké, Béké, he must be a cross between a Jew from Greenland and a peasant from the Auvergne.' A character called the Glazier, a wise workman who might have been borrowed from O'Casey, considers the name Beckett and remarks, 'Never heard of him. Seems he eats his soup with a fork.'[14] The prompter also arrives on stage in fury, throws down the script and walks out. Nowadays this jokey self-consciousness might appear old-hat in the theatre but it shows the measure of Beckett's confidence years before Joan Littlewood's Theatre Workshop.[15] In none other of Beckett's plays does he break up the illusion quite so deliberately. It has to be said that the material of the play badly needs this comic relief. For two years young Victor has lived alone in a bare room while his fond parents, the Kraps, and his flighty fiancée, rejoicing under the name Olga Skunk, fret about him and try to reclaim him. A new in-law, one Dr Piouk (dare one write 'sic' in brackets here?), advises that Victor be offered a fatal dose on the basis that the solution to the problem of consciousness 'simply consists in eliminating consciousness' (108). The Glazier insists that they have to find a meaning for Victor's world weariness in order to get him, as he puts it, 'tolerated' by society (105). Dr Piouk argues that if Victor refuses the suicide option, 'that has a meaning' (113), and if he accepts the pill that too has a meaning, namely, 'That he has had enough.' Everything, goes the Pioukish philosophy, 'aspires either to the black or to the white. Colour is syncopation' (113). Victor, however, does not want to be put into a black-and-white situation. Though he is as reluctant as Beckett the author to explain himself, under threat of Chinese torture Victor declares that what he wants is not to live the life set down as the one and only normal one. On the contrary, what he wants, and presumably what all of Beckett's alienated figures whether in novels or plays desire, is 'a life consumed by its own liberty' (147). Here the theme of the whole play and perhaps of Beckett's whole *oeuvre* comes out at last. 'At first,' Victor explains, 'I was a prisoner of other people. So I left them. Then I was a prisoner of myself. That was worse. So I left myself' (147). Asked how he achieved this somewhat mystical feat Victor, more sure of himself than most of Beckett's anti-heroes, obligingly replies: 'By being the least possible. By not moving, not thinking, not dreaming, not speaking, not listening, not perceiving, not knowing, not wishing, not being able, and so on. I believed that that was where my prisons lay' (149). He considers taking Dr Piouk's pill and then rejects it as a choice of genuine freedom, here employing for the first time Beckett's famous use of the pause on stage: 'My life will be long and horrible. [*pause*] But not so horrible as yours. [*pause*] I shall never be free. [*pause*] But I shall always feel that I am becoming free. [*pause*]' And so on for eight lines more. Having got rid of all those who have tried to rehabilitate him, including Mlle. Skunk, Victor pulls his bed close to the audience and lies down turning his emaciated back, as the final stage direction has it, on 'humanity' (170). This is a gesture far more obvious than Beckett was ever subsequently to make. He is clearly saying in 1947 that defiance is all, revolt *à la* Camus the only honest response to society as constituted. He has no desire to change that society; indeed, in spite of his part in the French Resistance during World War Two, Beckett did not believe change was possible. But the individual was free to be unfree in the world as constituted, let the Godots come or not come as they may.

So, where do we stand then in our attempt to come to terms with Beckett in his centenary year? We do not stand still at any rate. He himself did not stand still throughout the long years of his literary career. His work went through several phases, *All That Fall* marking one turning point and *Eleutheria* marking another. There are others as well: his first novel, *Murphy*, and the trilogy of novels in French marked different attempts to put Joyce behind him and write his own kind of fiction. Like his own heroes Beckett kept on in the face of overwhelming and often self-imposed difficulties, accepting that failure was part of the enterprise, for, as he put it, 'to be an artist is to fail, as no other dare fail', since 'failure is his world and to shrink from it desertion'.[16] So, too, it would appear, for the individual. It is a case of 'Nohow on' in spite of the conditions. It is a case of 'Try again. Fail again. Fail better,' as he put it in that late text *Worstword Ho*.[17] Perhaps this is what Patrick Kavanagh detected in Beckett's work when he remarked, 'The remedy is that Beckett has put despair and futility on the stage for us to laugh at them. And we do laugh.'[18] The *risus purus* turns out to be your only man. In the later work, to be sure, the laughter subsides and like the Fool in *King Lear* we are left darkling. But we are never left without the brio of the language, which, even in the ultimate situations Beckett imagines for us, ripples with dark humour. Dan Rooney in *All That Fall* declares that 'not even certified death' is equal to the pleasure of solitude and a good repast, implying that to be dead and conscious of it would be a supreme pleasure too (*CDW* 194). Maybe we should just finish our booze and leave it at that.

TERENCE
BROWN

Beckett and irish society

I n a meditation on the work of the Irish painter Jack Yeats, Samuel Beckett memorably stated: 'The artist who stakes his being is from nowhere, has no kith.'[1] In so doing he was bearing witness to the way in which great art seems to touch on universal themes, whatever its particular, local inspiration. In Jack Yeats Beckett saluted an artist whose concentration on figures in an Irish landscape or streetscape had broken free from mere representation to express fundamental truths about the human condition. In so evoking the achievement of his friend and fellow Irishman, Beckett powerfully reminds us that his own *oeuvre* gives an equivalent sense of an art that takes for its themes elemental, ineluctable aspects of human experience: the plastic nature of time in which to wait is to endure, the fading of powers in old age, the atemporal quality of memory as it inhabits past, present and future in a moment, the abiding presence of pain and the propinquity of laughter and anguish, the inextricable relationship of consciousness and language. It was to the universality of the work that the Nobel Prize committee drew attention when they awarded Samuel Beckett the prize for literature in 1969, making him the third Irishman to that date to be so honoured. They found in his writings 'a body of work that, in new forms of fiction and the theatre, has transmuted the destitution of modern man into his exaltation'.

Beckett of course, like Yeats, like us all, did not come from nowhere. Indeed it is a paradox of his literary method in various media that works which seem to present us with images shorn of a specific setting as voices come out of the dark from no place, from nowhere in an unremitting flow of words, often have their origin in obsessive acts of recollection of specific Irish places and times and of a vestigial social milieu. It is this that makes Beckett the laureate supreme of the vestigial itself and of the terminal.

It is worth calibrating fairly precisely Samuel Beckett's social origins in early twentieth-century Ireland to identify the kind of cultural ambiance in which the writer-to-be came to maturity, if only to wonder at how creativity can take apparently unfruitful material and make of it compelling literature. However, as I hope to suggest, knowledge of Beckett's background and experience in an Ireland undergoing major political change in his youth and young manhood can alert us to significant things about his work as a writer.

The Becketts were comfortably placed members of the Dublin Protestant middle class, which by the end of the nineteenth century was well established in the commercial life of the city – famously in brewing, whiskey distilling and in biscuit making. It is customary to speak in cultural critique and social history of 'the Anglo-Irish' or of the 'Protestant Ascendancy' as if these constituted a homogenous phenomenon in the midst of which Beckett can be readily situated. It is true, certainly, that the Becketts by reason of their Church of Ireland membership and conservative political outlook had lines of affiliation with powerful landholders and aristocratic families who were at the apex of social power in the land, but folk like the Becketts in Dublin and environs owed their success in life more to business acumen and professional worthiness than to inherited familial privilege or political entitlement (though ecclesiastic preferment could be a route to elevated social position in an Ireland where caste rather than class often affected prestige). Beckett's paternal ancestors were eighteenth-century Huguenot settlers in Dublin, where like many of their kind they prospered in the weaving trade. The writer's grandfather in partnership with a brother were highly successful building contractors, whose major works were those grand statements of Victorian civic responsibility, the National Library of Ireland and the Science and Art Museum, in Kildare Street. Beckett's own father, Bill, was an active, well-remunerated quantity surveyor. On the maternal side the Roes hailed from Leixlip, where a farming family with wealth generated by grain-milling found its fortunes at an ebb in the 1880s, so that when Beckett's father met May Roe, his wife-to-be, she was working as a nurse in the Adelaide Hospital in Dublin (which Bill Beckett's father's firm had in fact partly built). The Roe family home in Leixlip, when substantial riches had supported an ample domestic staff, had been named Cooldrinagh House. When Bill Beckett had an impressive Edwardian home built in the Tudor style in 1902 for himself and his pregnant wife in Foxrock in South County Dublin, he named it Cooldrinagh. It was as if he wished to assure his spouse that the proper order of things had been restored and that the future would be a stable and secure one for their offspring. A first son named Frank was born in 1902 and a second named Samuel on 13 April 1906.

In some ways the promise of that name, 'Cooldrinagh', was fulfilled. May Beckett, who forsook nursing for family life, turned her inherited energies to homemaking, which she oversaw with a highly developed sense of propriety and *politesse*. Her husband spent his time at work, on the golf course, on long walks and at the Kildare Street Club. She was a regular and devout church-goer, he just conventionally religious. Social life in the home was mostly a family affair. Summer holidays were spent in nearby Greystones, then a largely Protestant town where the Becketts could feel they were among their own. Sam's education was catered for locally until he was transferred to a private school in Dublin city. When he was thirteen he followed his brother as a boarding pupil at Portora Royal School in Enniskillen, County Fermanagh, a Church of Ireland establishment with traditions akin to those of the renowned English public schools. It was much favoured by the Protestant and Unionist professional classes for their sons (scions of the Ascendancy proper tended to be sent away to the English public schools, lest they retain Irish accents acquired at their Irish preparatory schools and from the servants). In 1923 Beckett matriculated at Trinity College, Dublin, where he would graduate with a first class degree in Modern Literature in October 1927 (examinations in those days fell in the autumn). And all of this could have assured May Beckett that God was in his heaven and all was right with the world again; but for the fact that seismic changes were taking place in Irish society at large that would, as the years passed, make the protected life of a Foxrock suburb with its Protestant decencies seem increasingly anachronistic and threatened.

Many of the Protestant Dublin middle class in the period after the 1916 Rising, when the partition of Ireland in 1920, the Anglo-Irish and civil wars and the establishment of the Irish Free State altered the country in ways most of them would have thought unimaginable a decade earlier, managed to remain apparently unaffected by the catclysm. Brian Inglis in his witty memoir *West Briton* (1962) recalled how in a seaside town to the north of Dublin, not unlike the world of Foxrock and Greystones inhabited by the Becketts, Protestant social life continued untroubled in the 1920s and 30s, despite all that had transpired. He remembered: 'Their social world remained stable; like a prawn in aspic, it gradually began to go stale, but it did not disintegrate. All around them "that other Ireland" as George Russell (AE) had called it, was coming into its force, but they remained almost unaware of its existence.'[2] However, for the Beckett family the kind of society that developed in the twenty-six counties of the Irish Free State after independence was to have a special effect upon them. For it helped to create the conditions in which their younger son would feel so deep an antipathy to the land of his birth that it in part accounts for his decision to abandon Dublin to make his life in Paris.

Trinity College also played its part in this process. When Beckett entered the college in 1923, with a not especially distinguished academic record, it was as a sportsman that he first made a name for himself. In his first year, in a remarkable achievement, he was chosen for the university's first eleven and his exploits on the cricket field were, as J.V. Luce has detailed, 'copiously documented in the sports pages of the *Irish Times* for the summer of 1924'.[3] His sporting father must have been delighted. As Beckett's university career progressed, however, grounds for concern arose. For the young sportsman at Trinity underwent the kind of intellectual awakening that can trouble relationships between the most sympathetic of parents and their offspring. Bill Beckett, hearty and outgoing, who rarely read anything other than adventure yarns, and the pious, moody and very proper May Beckett were ill-equipped to understand a son who, under the influence of a Francophile professor, became a proponent of literary avant-gardism and who veered alarmingly towards bohemianism in behaviour. The family connection had had, it is true, its complement of accomplished musicians and one of Beckett's aunts had attended art college in Dublin. These interests and accomplishments could be absorbed in the Low-Church Protestant ethos that was characteristic of their caste. A suspicion of literature, the French variety particularly suspect, whatever about music and painting, was never far from the surface in an Irish Protestant world that had been influenced by a puritan evangelicalism. Beckett's piously Protestant mother read little but the Bible and *The Irish Times*. As one of Beckett's biographers tells us, 'she declared that reading made her nervous'.[4] At university Samuel Beckett became a dedicate of literature; and of advanced forms of it at that.

The professorial mentor who helped to make of the cricketer a student of contemporary French literature, as Professor Roger Little has shown, was T.B. Rudmose-Brown. Rudmose-Brown was the London-born son of a Scots father and a Danish mother. Not only was he an acquaintance of living French writers, but also an individualist, an out-spoken freethinker in religion and an anticlerical (at a time when most Irish Protestants thought it prudent to keep silent on matters of church and state). His private life was irregular and his reputation was not unsullied. His attitude to the country in which he worked as a self-declared anti-imperialist was unsympathetic to the problems of the post-imperial. Authorial comments to a short story he published in the avant-garde Parisian periodical *transition* in 1927 suggest the measure of the man:

> You dare to say (what is obvious) that Ireland is the dirtiest country in the world, and the worst educated, that she cares nothing for art, is bound hand and foot to the Church, dares not think for herself [...]. The republicans are the worst enemies of freedom even in a country where no party, even perhaps no body at all, cares a 'tuppeny damn' about freedom, political or personal, and everybody, all parties talk incessantly about it, and commit all crimes against it in its name.[5]

In his 1934 collection of stories *More Pricks Than Kicks* Beckett was to include a recognisable and unflattering portrait of 'Ruddy' or 'Ruddy-nose' as he was known to generations of students; there he appeared as 'The Polar Bear, a big old brilliant lecher'.[6] It is beyond question, however, that the writer-to-be, as one of those students, absorbed many of Rudmose-Brown's attitudes in a process that not only set Beckett at odds with the respectable, prudent ethos of his family but placed him in opposition to the prevailing values of the country in which his parents hoped he would make his future.

Literature as an institution and as a practice was crucially involved in the life of the new Irish state and in ways that made it almost inevitable that Beckett would find himself alienated from that life. For the Rising of 1916 which set in motion the events that culminated in Irish independence in 1922 was in many ways a literary affair, a thing of symbolism and theatricality. Indeed, when the poet and dramatist W.B. Yeats was awarded the Nobel Prize for literature in 1923, in a lecture on the Irish Dramatic Movement, he had claimed that 'the modern literature of Ireland' had been a part of a general national stirring that had begun after the death of Parnell in 1891 and that had 'prepared for the Anglo-Irish war'.[7] In so speaking he was merely endorsing a general sentiment that literature and national identity in Ireland were intimately linked and that the Irish Literary Revival had played a role in making Ireland (or at least part of it) free. As an ex-pupil of Rudmose-Brown, who had extended his knowledge of radical literary French experiment in preparation for writing his monograph on Proust in 1930, Beckett could have none of that. His sense of a literary vocation was rooted in a conviction that the twentieth century had seen a fundamental alteration in human consciousness that only such writers as Proust and Joyce had expressed. To take the idea seriously that literature should involve itself with something as provincial as the nation or a national tradition would be to betray that calling. In an essay published in *The Bookman* in 1934 Beckett wrote of the twentieth-century context to which literature was required to respond in terms that bespeak impatient contempt for the Irish Literary Revival and especially for those who as late as the 1930s would seek to sustain its nationally minded project. For Beckett a 'rupture in the lines of communication' had taken place:

> Those who are not aware of the rupture, or in whom the velleity of becoming so was suppressed as a nuisance at its inception, will continue to purvey those articles which, in Ireland at least, had ceased to be valid even before the literary advisers to J.M. Synge found themselves prematurely obliged to look elsewhere for a creative hack. These are the anti-quarians, delivering with the altitudinous complacency of the Victorian Gael the Ossianic goods.[8]

Beckett's disdain for the Literary Revival and the nationalism it had helped to foster found humorous expression in his novel of 1938, *Murphy*. In that work Oliver Sheppard's statue of Cuchulain, erected in the General Post Office in 1935, site of where in 1916 Yeatsian dreams had borne fruit, is the butt of coarse comedy. Less humorous in the book is the scarcely disguised, venomous portrait of the poet Austin Clarke, one of the antiquarians of *The Bookman* essay. In *Murphy* he appears as Austin Ticklepenny, the 'Pot Poet from the County Dublin'.[9]

Beckett objected then to the way literature in Ireland was, as he saw it, expected to deliver 'the Ossianic goods', and was almost required to trade in what he unfairly discerned as Clarke's 'fully licensed stock-in trade, from Aisling to Red Branch Bundle'.[10] He also was repelled by the way Irish society saw fit to make literature a front in a moral and cultural war, with the Censorship of Publications Act of 1929 a peculiarly nasty weapon in that struggle.

It is one of the grim ironies of Irish history that a national movement for political independence, in which literature had served as an inspiring force, should have had as one of its outcomes a draconian literary censorship. This was put in place by the Censorship of Publications Act of 1929. This blunt legislative instrument was an expression of a variety of social forces. It was in part an attempt by government to meet the challenge of literary mass production in the English-speaking world, with many in the international community fearing societal pollution by grossly pornographic work. But it also reflected a fairly wide Irish consensus that a Catholic and Gaelic nation possessed a distinctive identity that must be protected from contamination by alien and especially English influences. Works of literature that dealt in any kind of sexual irregularity or made reference to the sexual act in any but the vaguest of terms quickly found themselves under interdiction. That the Censorship Act was more than simply an attempt to protect the Irish population from pornography is made even more clear by the fact that works which advocated 'the unnatural prevention of conception' were also made subject to censorship.

As might have been expected, Beckett was scornful of the literary censorship, and his own writings were to suffer a fate shared by that of such fellow countrymen as Seán O'Faoláin, Frank O'Connor, Liam O'Flaherty and Kate O'Brien in the

1930s, '40s and '50s. *More Pricks Than Kicks* and his novels *Watt* and *Molloy* were banned. The Beckettian response was sarcasm and derisive humour. He particularly noted the Act's proscription of works advocating contraception. In 1934 he wrote an article for *The Bookman* entitled 'Censorship and the *Saorstat*' (which was not published at that time). There, as Anthony Cronin notes, Beckett in a somewhat dutiful exercise of 'unrelieved sarcasm' saw accurately that 'the essence of the act and its exciting cause were the prohibitions of publications advocating the use of contraceptives'.[11] In *Watt*, the novel he wrote in unoccupied France during the Second World War, the cultural exclusiveness of Free State Ireland and its assertion of a Catholic and Gaelic identity, which involved the proscription of contraception, are subjected to withering satire. A research field trip in the Gaelic West is prefaced by a fantasy in which a product named 'Bando' is celebrated as a consistently dependable aphrodisiac:

> The unfortunate thing about Bando [...] is that it is no longer to be obtained in this unfortunate country [...] for Bando even on a Saturday afternoon, you will grovel in vain. For the State, taking as usual the law into its own hands, and duly indifferent to the sufferings of thousands of men, and tens of thousands of women, all over the country, has seen fit to place an embargo on this admirable article, from which joy could stream, at a moderate cost, into homes, and other places of rendez-vous, now desolate.[12]

In a short piece written a few years later, humour becomes Swiftian vituperation. In *First Love* the narrator opines, 'What constitutes the charm of our country, apart of course from its scant population, and this without help of the meanest contraceptive, is that all is derelict, with the sole exception of history's ancient faeces.'[13]

A desolate home, an even more desolate rendezvous and an imagery of dereliction are the substance of the work in which Beckett most directly addressed his immediate Irish background. This was the radio play *All That Fall*, first broadcast by the BBC in 1957. In this atmospheric piece, which exploited sound effects to compelling effect, Beckett evoked the South County Dublin world of his boyhood; but in the play it is that world imagined as eking out an exiguous existence in the context of post-independence Ireland (the signage on public conveniences is now in Irish). Life still goes on as always; the man of the house goes up to Dublin to his place of business. His wife is en route to meet him at the little station near a race-track. Weekly church worship is the expected thing. Suburban evenings are spent at home reading popular fiction. However in *All That Fall* such regularity of life is seen through a lens of black comedy and grim horror. Dan Rooney is no benign family man, but a blind misanthrope, inclined to infanticide (the plot of the play, such as it is, hinges on whether or not he has been involved in the death of a child which has delayed his train). Maddy Rooney, his wife, is haunted by the death of her own, possibly imaginary, child in a play in which sterility, illness and mortality are almost *dramatis personae*. The effect is to suggest terminal states, a social milieu without the resources to reproduce itself in a context in which all things are subject to inexorable decay. The ditches are full of rotting autumnal leaves although the month is June. Dan thinks Maddy speaks as if she is struggling with a dead language. 'Well, you know,' she observes, 'it will be dead in time, just like our own poor Gaelic, there is that to be said.'[14] The play is framed by the strains of the melancholic slow movement of Schubert's string quartet 'Death and the Maiden'. A remembered Ireland here, quite directly invoked in its social constituents, is made to express an appalled vision of life that admits of no palliatives for decay, loss and death. As such it alerts us to how Dublin and its environs recurrently if much less directly exists as a kind subterranean imaginary place in almost all of Beckett's work, at once available in memory and at the same time victim to change and dereliction, at once present in recalled particulars and then absent except as it can be textually recreated in language, which like our own poor Gaelic will also be dead in time.

'There was never any city but the one,' states the narrator in a story Beckett wrote in 1946.[15] For him that city was Dublin, with its mountains, its two canals, its sea and islands, all, as J.C.C. Mays has noted, apprehended in his writings as a child might see it from his home district with 'distances ... collapsed and distorted'.[16] In that way in his writings it becomes a mythic city of the mind, a primal place remembered not in nostalgia, though nostalgia is certainly present at times, nor to offer the consolation of a recalled stability, but to be recollected in a mode of consciousness in which that consciousness is aware of its own utterly mysterious placelessness in time. And such memory of things past is a measure of the radical displacement of the artist who stakes his being, who has no kith.

GERRY DUKES

the godot phenomenon

Beckett wrote *En attendant Godot* in Paris, beginning on 9 October 1948 and concluding on 29 January 1949. The manuscript is contained in one notebook – a graph-paper school exercise copybook to be precise – which has not been generally available for inspection by scholars and academics. By all the accounts that have so far been produced the manuscript is clean and continuous with little evidence of hesitation or difficulty in the composition. This feature renders it very different from Beckett's novels or novellas in manuscript, many of which display, in the form of complex and complicated doodles and the like, that Beckett did not often experience the kind of ease of composition that characterises the manuscript of *En attendant Godot*. By Beckett's own account there were 'several' more stages to the compositional process[1] before the first published edition of the play was issued by the Paris publisher, Les Éditions de Minuit, in October 1952.

The play opened at the Théâtre de Babylone in January 1953 and was greeted initially with some incomprehension and hostility. The players soldiered on and gradually the play acquired a cult status and became the 'must see' of the theatrical season. Barney Rosset of Grove Press in New York had already commissioned from Beckett a translation of the novel *Molloy* which Minuit had published in 1951 and, now that *En attendant Godot* was making a noise in the world, he began to press Beckett for a translation of the play. Beckett was unwilling to take it on because he was working intensively with the South African Paul Bowles on the translation of *Molloy* and he was also collaborating with Elmar Tophoven, a young German teacher who was working in Paris, on a translation of the play into German. The exact nature of this collaboration is not fully known yet but we may surmise that it arose from the fact that Tophoven's draft translation had used the Minuit 1952 edition as base text. While participating in the rehearsal process with the director Roger Blin (Blin also played Pozzo) Beckett had introduced numerous cuts, changes and the like to the text and he was committed to carrying the changes he made to the French text over to the German translation.

By late June 1953, however, Beckett had found the time to translate his play and he sent a copy to Barney Rosset at Grove Press and to various theatrical agencies in England and the United States. In an accompanying letter to Rosset he described the translation as 'rushed' and expressed his dissatisfaction with it.[2] Nevertheless he undertook to revise his translation as soon as he could find the time. He travelled to Berlin in September for the première of *Wir Warten auf Godot* (as the play was then titled). In fact, by the time he got around to revising his 'rushed' version in November and December of 1953 between five and eight separate productions of his play were running in theatres across the Federal Republic of West Germany. The ironies cannot have been lost on Beckett, that one-time activist in the French Resistance – having struggled as a full-time writer, first in English and since 1945 in French, he became an overnight success in German.

The success of *Godot* in Germany should not surprise us. The Second World War, the dismemberment of Germany itself into East and West, the Nuremberg Trials, the Berlin Airlift, the beginning of the Cold War and the Marshall Aid programme were all recent events not yet forgotten, occluded or assuaged by post-war economic recovery. The figure of Pozzo, for example, with his unctuous assumption of superiority and exercise of arbitrary cruelty, would have resonated powerfully with a German audience. But *Godot* has resonated with audiences around the world and in many languages and continues to do so to this day. So we are dealing with a phenomenon that is not tied into particular or specific social or historical circumstances even though the play may well have its origins in Beckett's own experiences during the Second World War, as is evidenced by a small number of very specific details to be found in the original French version of the play. The references to the Ariège, to the river Durance, to the wine-maker Bonnelly just outside the village of Roussillon in the Vaucluse (where, as Vladimir says in the second act, 'Mais là-bas tout est rouge!' – 'But down there everything is red!') all gesture towards landscapes and people that Beckett came to know as he hid from the Gestapo for over two years. Beckett, however, chose to cut or change these specifics in the translation into English.

It was the late Vivian Mercier who memorably described *Godot* as a play in which 'nothing happens, twice'. This is far more than a smart critical remark; it is a profound insight into the very heart of Beckett's achievement in the play. For by the time he came to write *Waiting for Godot* Beckett's conception of what a play could be or should be had changed radically. A play is not designed to tell a story, point a moral or recruit its audience to a point of view, still less to a conviction or even an opinion. This had not always been the case. In the first two months of 1947 Beckett wrote (in French) his first full-length three-act play titled *Eleutheria* (the word means freedom in Greek). Copies of this play were circulating among theatrical producers in Paris at the same time as *Godot* was doing the same rounds. There were one or two expressions of interest in the play and Beckett even signed a contract for publication by

Minuit. At the eleventh hour, so to speak, Beckett broke his contract with Minuit and refused to allow publication. That refusal stood right up to just before his death in 1989 when he insisted to Jérôme Lindon of Minuit that it was not to be published, even in the context of a projected *Complete Works*. Nevertheless, for reasons far too convoluted to go into here, the play has since been published in French and has been translated into English twice.[3] *Eleutheria* is a curious work, more debate than drama. Its central character Victor Krap has retreated to a squalid bed-sit where he spends his time doing nothing and striving to be free and where he is intensively visited by many others – members of his family and their servants, his fiancée Olga Skunk, a glazier and his son. A spectator from the audience also gets in on the act, as does a Chinese torturer. In fact, *Eleutheria* anticipates by some years the kinds of situations and actions that came to be labelled as the Theatre of the Absurd. It is legitimate, if idle, to speculate what the impact would have been on Beckett's subsequent career as a writer if he had allowed publication of the play or had found a producer willing to take on the play that requires two sets – one of which has to be brushed aside into the orchestra pit for the third act – and seventeen members of cast. *Eleutheria* mixes French farce, vaudeville routines and slapstick comedy with some rather fraught and personal materials. It is my guess that he came to regard the mix as indigestible and simply withdrew the play. He gifted a copy of his typescript of the play to the American academic Lawrence Harvey in the sixties when Harvey was engaged on a critical study of Beckett's work as poet and critic.[4] Later, in the eighties, he allowed a lengthy excerpt from the play to be published in a special number of the *Revue d'Esthétique* published to mark his eightieth birthday.[5] At around this time he also undertook to translate the play for Barney Rosset, who had run into some business difficulties, but he gave up the task, as he said at the time, 'in disgust'.

What is literally astonishing about *Waiting for Godot* is that it is assembled out of very similar materials – comic turns, pratfalls, vaudeville – but to much different effect and all deployed within a much tighter two-act structure. The principal difference between *Eleutheria* and *Waiting for Godot* is that the latter play has no point of view, it has nothing to say. This becomes very clear if we consider for a moment the play's pre-history. In late 1951 or early 1952, before publication in October of that year and ahead of the first performance in January 1953, Beckett's typescript was submitted to an office of the French Ministry of Education. There it was assessed and considered worthy of a small grant to assist it towards theatrical production. A radio producer with Radiodiffusion Française (a state-owned radio station) by the name of Michel Polac had access to all scripts that had attracted Ministry grants and he featured some of these in a bi-monthly radio programme. The programme usually consisted of selected scenes from the play performed after a brief introduction to the play by a critic or scholar and a statement about the work from its author. Beckett did in fact provide a statement but he deputed Roger Blin to read it on-air. The full text of Beckett's statement is carried on the back jacket of the current Minuit printing of *En attendant Godot*.[6] It has also been translated into English twice,[7] but not by Beckett. He claims that he put everything he knew about the characters and their situations into the play, that he knew next to nothing about the theatre, that the arrival of Pozzo and Lucky in both acts must have been arranged so as to break the monotony for the on-stage pair, Vladimir and Estragon.

In claiming to know next to nothing about the theatre Beckett was being economical with the truth. While he lived in rooms at Trinity College, first as a student in the twenties and then as a junior academic in the early thirties, he availed, on a regular basis, of opportunities to attend the Queen's and Abbey theatres and variety shows at the Royal and Olympia. His published criticism from the thirties and references in some of his letters all demonstrate a level of conversancy with theatre and plays in excess of the merely amateur. And, of course, he had helped to write and had performed in George Pelorson's spoof version of Corneille's *Le Cid* for Trinity's Modern

Language Association at the Peacock Theatre, part of the Abbey Theatre, while he was a junior academic in Trinity in the early thirties. It is fair to say that he knew quite a bit about theatre before writing *Godot* and he put that knowledge to extraordinarily good use in writing the play.

The setting for the first act of *Godot* could hardly be less specific: *A country road. A tree. Evening.* The second act is set: *Next day. Same time. Same place.* The play is set nowhere in particular, which is tantamount to saying it can be set almost anywhere. This feature alone highlights the 'exportable' quality of the play; it is 'at home' wherever it is played. The scenic requirements are minimal – a suggestion of road, a bare tree in the first act (with the addition of a few bright green leaves for the second), a low mound (or a stone, according to the change that Beckett introduced for the production he directed at the Schiller Theater in Berlin in 1975). For the moon-rise that heralds the imminent end of both acts in that production Beckett specified a pale blue spotlight mounted on the end of a lever mechanism that inscribed a slow quarter circle as it rose behind the cyclorama that constituted the backcloth. The effect was eerie and cold and wonderfully theatrical because when the moon attained its full elevation it swayed gently for some moments, allowing the audience to intuit the nature of the mechanism that had hoisted the lamp. We should mention that the Gate Theatre production that will play in London and Dublin this centenary year is a very close relative of that 1975 Schiller production because the director, Walter Asmus, was Beckett's assistant in Berlin. Since that time Asmus has directed *Godot* numerous times and in quite a few languages and has found that the closer he keeps to Beckett's prescriptions the greater the expressive freedoms he and his casts can access. Beckett's own experience in the theatre impressed upon him the validity of the modernist aesthetic that less is always more, that the tighter the constraints the greater the urge to transcend them. In 1982 he turned this insight into a play called *Catastrophe* and dedicated it to a fellow playwright, Vaclav Havel, who was then undergoing the severe constraint of imprisonment.

Let's consider for a moment Beckett's approach to his characters, Vladimir and Estragon. He provides them with, at most, a very sketchy past. We are told that 'a million years ago, in the nineties' they were 'presentable' (the rushed 1953 version has 'respectable'), they both wear bowler hats – those relics of old decency also worn by Pozzo and Lucky – and when Vladimir tells Estragon he should have been a poet Estragon responds by saying: 'I was. [*Gesture towards his rags.*] Isn't that obvious.' So the pair have been together for a long time; they have come down in the world; they have worked as grape harvesters; they have no fixed abode – Estragon spent the night before 'in a ditch' where he was beaten 'as usual'. The play does not disclose where Vladimir spends his nights; all we can say is that the two men part company and meet again the following day, hence the semi-elaborate, almost ceremonial embraces exchanged at the beginning of both acts. While their past is sketchy their present admits of very low definition as well. As for their future, they have hopes of help and assistance from a man called Godot with whom or with one of his agents they have made an appointment to meet at the tree by the side of the road.

The appointment, however, like much else in the play, is contaminated by uncertainty. They are not sure that the tree they wait at is the right tree; they are unsure as to the precise date and time appointed but they are sure that if they fail to keep the appointment Godot or his agents will punish them. Nevertheless, towards the end of each act Godot or his agents dispatch a messenger to the waiting two to tell them that he cannot come today but surely tomorrow. The boy who delivers the message is the same in both acts though in the second act he denies this, suggesting that the earlier messenger may have been his brother. One of the clear inferences to be drawn from Godot's deferral of the appointment is, as the cliché insists, that tomorrow never comes, it turns into today as a new one forms just over time's horizon, a threshold we can never cross. In one of his more piercing moments of lucidity in the first act Vladimir says of himself and Estragon that they have got rid of their rights. By making their endlessly deferred appointment they have effectively given themselves over to the power (if that is what it is) of the invisible Godot. All they can do in this circumstance is wait and while waiting endeavour to keep themselves entertained. This becomes increasingly difficult and fraught as their resources shrink and dwindle, waste and pine while the play takes its course so that the arrival of the other pair, Pozzo and Lucky, comes as a very welcome diversion. When they return in the second act the now blind Pozzo is led by Lucky on a much abbreviated rope. Lucky stops short at the sight of the other two, Pozzo blunders into him and knocks him down, Pozzo falls too and the pair sprawl on the stage, surrounded by the scattered baggage. Vladimir's response is interesting: 'Reinforcements at last!' he says. 'Now we're sure to see the evening out.' Remembering the original title of the play, *En attendant Godot*, we now see that Vladimir and Estragon are, to use a French term, *attentistes*, literally those who wait.

The term had widespread currency in France during the war, especially among those who were active in the Resistance, not only in the German occupied territory but also in the Unoccupied Zone administered by the indigenous puppet fascist regime of Marshal Pétain. The term was hostile when it was not merely contemptuous and designated those who were content to put up with their circumstances, to grin and bear it, so to speak. Beckett was not one of those: he was active in Paris during the occupation and, after the security of the cell he worked for was breached and he fled south with his partner, he volunteered for the local *maquis* in the Vaucluse. Beckett was decorated by the provisional French government after the war but he insisted that his participation in the Resistance was 'boy scout stuff'. That may have been the case but many other non-nationals who had been active in the Resistance did not survive the war. Beckett chose to resist rather than to remain an *attentiste*, just as he chose to participate in the effort of the Irish Red Cross at the so-called Irish Hospital in the flattened town of Saint-Lô from August 1945 to the end of January in 1946. Unlike the vast majority of his fellow Irishmen Beckett chose active resistance and participation in the post-war reconstruction rather than the insular neutrality that allowed them to be (as he put it some years later) 'simply limply republican'.[8]

Beckett's distaste for authoritarianism, in all of its forms, is made manifest in the Pozzo/Lucky relationship. Initially this relationship seems straightforwardly brutal and cruel. Lucky, with a rope around his neck that tethers him to Pozzo, is burdened with baggage and is literally driven by Pozzo who is equipped with a whip. So Pozzo is a slave-driver and Lucky is his slave. During the lengthy passage of dialogue in the first act about why Lucky does not put down the bags even while he is at rest, Pozzo states that Lucky 'carries like a pig,' 'it is not his job' and that he is bringing him to the fair where he hopes to get a good price for him. Vladimir's initial response is conventional: "To treat a man ... like that ... I think that ... no ... a human being ... no ... it's a scandal!' And yet when Pozzo philosophises about the constant quantity of tears and laughter in the world he claims that he has gleaned these insights from Lucky, from whom he has learnt of 'Beauty, grace, truth of the first water.' A moment later he complains that the way Lucky goes on is intolerable and is 'killing' him. Vladimir, fickle as public opinion, rounds on Lucky: 'How dare you! It's abominable! Such a good master! Crucify him like that! After so many years! Really!' Six utterances punctuated by six exclamation marks, the final one the weakest of the set, suggest that Vladimir's initial response was merely knee-jerk and this one is as well. Vladimir's moral outrage directed towards Pozzo is easily redirected towards Lucky. If that is the case then his moral outrage is merely journalistic; it cannot be genuine.

It is the unfortunate, abused, burdened and exploited Lucky who, nevertheless, is permitted to deliver a speech which, though disjointed, fragmented, assembled from the remnants of various branches of wisdom and knowledge, articulates unpalatable truths about the human condition. Farcical authorities are cited, the 'Acacacacademy of Anthropopopometry' – that seat of wind and spatter – is invoked but the fact remains that man inevitably 'shrinks and dwindles', 'wastes and pines' despite the advances in 'alimentation and defecation', nutrition and waste management. We live in 'an abode of stones' that are more perdurable than we are – they were here before us and they will abide long after we have gone. While Lucky speaks the others become increasingly agitated and disquieted. All three throw themselves on Lucky and, when his hat is removed, he falls silent at last.

The return of Pozzo and Lucky in the second act is alarming, to say the least. Lucky is now dumb – he cannot even groan – and Pozzo is blind, or so he says. The pair seem to exist in a different order of time where to 'shrink and dwindle' are processes which have been accelerated, where degeneration and attrition are ineluctable. Lucky, who was driven by Pozzo, now leads him. The whirligig of time brings in his revenges. Pozzo, who in the first act consulted his watch so as finically to observe his schedule, now fulminates against 'accursed time'. His summarising image: 'They give birth astride the grave, the light gleams an instant, then it's night once more,' is as pithy, as depressing as anything in the Old Testament.

Beckett was disturbed by the fuss and confusion (his terms) generated by his play in the fifties and beyond. His view was simple, even programmatic. A playwright composes a script; it is then realised in rehearsal with a director and cast and a technical crew. It is finally created in performance with a live audience. It is the audience that is the final creative ingredient or agent that completes the work. Beckett warmed to this notion in a letter to the American theatre director Alan Schneider in December 1957: 'My work is a matter of fundamental sounds (no joke intended), made as fully as possible, and I accept responsibility for nothing else. If people want to have headaches among the overtones, let them. And provide their own aspirin.'[9] *Godot* has been particularly productive in inducing interpretative headaches. It has been seen as a post-holocaust play, a Christian allegory, a pessimistic fable, a nihilistic cry of despair, an indictment of an absconded God and, for the producer of its first American outing in

Miami (of all places), 'the laugh sensation of two continents'. It is all of these things and none of them. It is what the members of the audience make of it, what they bring to it. *Waiting for Godot* is the mirror of your conscience.

DECLAN KIBERD

murphy and the world of samuel beckett

A medical friend once took Samuel Beckett for a walk in the Dublin hills, hoping to cheer him up. 'It's a beautiful day,' said the friend. 'Oh, it's all right,' grunted the writer. 'No, it's the sort of day that makes you glad to be alive,' insisted the medic, to which Beckett snapped, 'I wouldn't go that far.'[1]

The young artist saw life as a disease, a loss of immortality. Much of the comedy in his world derives from this fish–out-of-water condition, when people are suddenly caught at some disadvantage out of their appropriate role. In Beckett's works, people who regain consciousness do not 'come to' – rather they 'come from'. 'You saved my life,' says a character in his early novel *Murphy* (1938), as if this is a terrible crime: 'now palliate it.'[2] To his dying day, Beckett claimed to be able to recall life in the womb and the trauma of his birth. He felt at times that he had not been fully born, arguing that his inability to get out of bed or out of his mother's house was proof of a womb fixation.

All of this finds an echo not just in the character of Murphy, but also in that of his acquaintance, Cooper, who cannot take off his hat because 'the memories it awoke of the caul were too painful' (69). *Murphy* the novel is set in London, to which Beckett moved in the 1930s after a nervous collapse. He found the transition from Dublin painful. At home, he had been treated as an educated gentleman from a good Protestant family; in England he was just another Paddy, so that even simple acts like ordering a meal or buying a paper left him vulnerable to feelings of ridicule. All of this time, Beckett's family tried to goad him into gainful employment, as Celia in the book cajoles her lover Murphy; but he preferred an idle life, mixing with bohemians and prostitutes, saying that he wanted to lie on his back, fart and just think about Dante.

Murphy is a novel of emigration, an attempt to document the plight of those Irish in England who have to contest the image of the Stage Paddy at every turn. Referred to as 'the ruins of the ruins of the broth of a boy' (126), Murphy appears to English onlookers as a bedraggled moron, all body, but his real problem is that he is to himself all mind. He sees himself very justly as a sophisticated, angst-ridden intellectual, but when he goes looking for manual labour, he is mocked as a buffoon. He decides that there is no point in trying to break down the closed system that is the English stereotype of Irishness in 1930s London.

All of Beckett's world is built on closed systems. Murphy's mind is such a system, impenetrable by anyone, even his lover Celia; and so any real form of communication is found to be impossible. The ultimate closed system for Beckett is language itself, used throughout the book to obscure rather than illuminate reality. A character named Quigley is 'a well-to-do ne'er-do-well' (14) and the very circularity of the hyphenated phrases underlines the sense of hopelessness. Great play is made of the similarities between the name Celia and the French phrase 's'il y a' (68) but nobody can extract any meaning from the sad pun. It is like a Zen *koan*, something which can only cripple or exhaust the mind which seeks illumination from it.

The novel itself opens with an account of the entire universe as an impermeable code: 'The sun shone, having no alternative, on the nothing new.' A subsequent sentence cuts to Murphy's tragedy of self-deception: 'Murphy sat out of it, as though he were free, in a mew in West Brompton' (5). His error is to believe that he can opt out of this world and attain freedom in his pure mind. Though communication may be impossible, Beckett persists in the belief that other people are still necessary, if only to provide us with a measure of our solitude. There may be self-exile but there is no self-sufficiency.

But Murphy falsely believes that there is and so he sits in his rocking-chair in a daily attempt to find it. The rocking appeases his body, so that he can come alive in the mind. 'And life in his mind gave him pleasure, such pleasure that pleasure was not the word' (6). That cliché will be repeated as an instance of how threadbare phrases can be so worn down as to defeat all communication. Murphy himself is a closed system and great play is made of his non-porous suit, which prevents internal air from escaping or external air from entering, with disastrous results in terms of body odour.

The comedy of non-communication is developed in many ways. Murphy's guru is the Cork mystic Neary, whose surname may be an anagram for 'yearn', but who finds himself just a single link in a chain of futile, star-crossed lovers:

Of such was Neary's love for Miss Dwyer, who loved a
Flight-Lieutenant Elliman, who loved a Miss Farren of
Ringaskiddy, who loved a father Fitt of Ballinclashet,
who in all sincerity was bound to acknowledge a certain
vocation for a Mrs West of Passage, who loved Neary. (7)

The circuit of emotion returns to Neary, but not in a manner which satisfies his or anyone else's desire.

A similar farce of non-reciprocation is developed in much of the novel's dialogue. Typographically, the pages look as if they record conversations, but often upon inspection reveal that it is one person who does all the talking:

'Liar,' said Wylie.

This was not a question. Cooper waited for the next question.

'Neary knows too much,' said Wylie.

Cooper waited.

'You split on him,' said Wylie, 'he splits on you. Isn't that it?' Cooper admitted nothing.

'All you need,' said Wylie, 'is a little kindness, and in a short time you will be sitting down and taking off your hat and doing all the things that are impossible at present.' (72)

Such passages are effectively soliloquies. They point forward to the monologues of *Molloy* or *Malone Dies*, as well as to the later short plays. The obsession with monologue may be rooted in Beckett's Church of Ireland background, for the Protestant confession is made ultimately to the self, on the basis that every man is his own priest. Because the self can never fully shrive and forgive the self, such monologue is, as Hugh Kenner has said, issueless and potentially endless.[3]

All through *Murphy*, silence is proposed as mankind's destiny. 'Avoid exhaustion by speech' is the counsel given to Murphy on a handbill passed to him by a swami; and the novel might well be read as an almost eastern espousal of quietism. For Murphy, the only way to conquer desire is to ablate it. Silence is his fourth highest attribute; and he ends one chapter listening spellbound to the dead line on a dangling telephone. As the plot unfolds, the many forms of language either stumble or fail completely. Even the terse language of a cryptic telegram becomes confusing: 'LOST STOP STOP WHERE YOU ARE STOP COOPER' (36).

Slips of the tongue are endless. 'O reary, Neilly' for 'O really, Neary' or 'Sog. I mean fog'. For his part, Murphy's associate Wylie abandons language as a futile medium when compared with the greater eloquence of bodily gesture, most often a shrug 'that he always used when words were inadequate to conceal what he felt' (75). Beckett well understood the meaning of Oscar Wilde's witticism that everybody is good until they learn how to talk. This ability to obfuscate with words is seen as a particularly Irish gift. When Neary, maddened with unfulfilled desire, tries to dash out his brains on the buttocks of the statue of Cuchulain in the GPO, a Garda says with supreme tautology to the crowd which had gathered to witness the event: 'Move on, [...] before yer moved on' (29). The narrator adds: 'It was not in the CG's nature to bandy words, nor had it come into any branch of his training.'

This is true also of Wylie, who shares with many Irish politicians the ability to rob his own sentences of the meaningful climax of a finite verb:

> 'I nearly forgot to say,' he said, 'that when you see Miss Counihan – you will be seeing her, won't you Cooper?'
>
> The skill is really extraordinary with which analphabetes, especially those of Irish education, circumvent their dread of verbal commitments. Now Cooper's face, though it did not seem to move a muscle, brought together and threw off in a single grimace the finest shades of irresolution, revulsion, doglike devotion, catlike discretion, fatigue, hunger, thirst and reserves of strength, in a very small portion of the time that the finest oratory would require for a grossly inferior evasion, and without exposing its proprietor to misquotation. (115)

That long sentence not only suggests that bodily language cannot be misquoted – it also, more significantly, reads like an extended stage direction. It expresses discontent with the limited capacity of words to capture states of feeling and re-inforces that sense of discontent with many flashbacks, flashes forward and interpolations. You get the impression of an artist who is straining at the leash in his attempt to break through the conventions of the novel form, in an art which is already half-way to drama, the genre which many years later would ensure Beckett's lasting fame.

On many occasions the narrator breaks down the illusion which has been built up in *Murphy* and he does this with interpolated stage directions. In Chapter Ten, for instance, Neary accidentally kicks a hot-water bottle out of his bed and it bursts, 'so that water is oozing towards the centre of the floor throughout the scene that follows' (117). If *Murphy* is the finest modern attempt to subject the figure of the Stage Irishman to the close psychological analysis made possible by the novel form, then these stagy effects are all the more appropriate as carry-overs from theatre. Many of the exchanges in the book read as if the characters were going through an oft-rehearsed set of speeches:

> 'Everywhere I find defiled,' continued Miss Counihan, 'in the crass and unharmonious unison, the mind at the cart-tail of the body, the body at the chariot-wheels of the mind. I name no names.'
> 'Excellent reception,' said Wylie.
> 'No trace of fading,' said Neary. (122)

This anticipates Pozzo's theatrical description of the sunset in *Waiting for Godot*, as well as his apology at the close: 'I faded a little towards the end.'[4] The narrator of *Murphy* says that all his characters, with the exception of Murphy, are puppets; but that narrator himself seems to be the ultimate puppet, trapped by his pre-existing story into performing a pre-ordained role, as when he apologises for what he must do next – 'It is most unfortunate, but the point of this story has been reached where a justification of the expression "Murphy's Mind" has to be attempted' (63). In this way, he shrugs off his duty to propel the plotline forward, even as he seems to submit to his duty to provide a continuing narrative.

The narrator is clearly apologetic and ill at ease in the role, constantly referring to his own problems with the censors or to the difficulties which the typographer will have setting up some capitalised lettering. It is as if the narrator has severe doubts about the validity of the story *and* about his own capacity to find the right words to tell it. What we are offered in the end is not so much a novel written by an author as an imitation of a novel narrated by a man who is nervously impersonating the kind of author he thinks he ought to be. Like all of Beckett's characters, he also feels himself caught between a role and a self. As a novelist he is so unsure that he often lapses into the dramatic form, with stage directions, rehearsed soliloquies and so on. He and his characters are trapped by a script whose words they did not write and by a novel form in which he is fast losing faith: "'If you have news of my love," said Miss Counihan, "speak, speak, I adjure you." She was an omnivorous reader' (69).

Nobody can recall the full script, whose meaning is not wholly understood. In that sense, they all seem like modern puppets who have cut the strings which once bound them to God and are therefore left stranded in centre-stage, trying to hold down a role. With the death or loss of God, man seems reduced to inauthentic being and all actions become stagy and hollow, once the divine source of significance is removed. Hence that very modern feeling of a life lived in quotation marks, of being the performer of a role which is understood only by someone else. In Beckett's world, people no longer assert a position, but simply endure a fate.

This novel *Murphy* itself seems to exist in inverted commas, or, as the structuralists would say, perverted commas, being an apologetic recycling of clichés by an author who has no freedom to choose any others but cannot fail to notice their inadequacy. He is a creature of a literary tradition in which he is losing faith. Hence his ferocious parody of a famous passage in James Joyce's *A Portrait of the Artist as a Young Man* where Stephen Dedalus says, 'It was very big to think about everything and everywhere. Only God could do that.'[5] Now, Murphy wonders about the gas fire that will finally take his life: 'Gas. Could it turn a neurotic into a psychotic? No. Only God could do that' (100). Such jibes are based in a sense of despair about the truth-telling powers of literature, as when Neary says cynically to Wylie: 'Let our conversation now be without precedent in fact or literature, each one speaking to the best of his ability the truth to the best of his knowledge' (120). Beckett has in fact so little faith in the power of literature or language that he locates the climax of his novel in a chess-game.

The ultimate indictment of language, however, is the strangely moving but unsatisfactory relationship between Murphy and Celia. 'Celia loved Murphy, Murphy loved Celia, it was a striking case of love requited' (13).

In bed together their heads face opposite ways but they touch beautifully in what the narrator calls 'the short circuit so earnestly desired by Neary' (21). Neary, however, can achieve it only within the closed system of his solitary body, by keeping his toes touching like terminals as he harmonises his yin and yang. This is Beckett's early warning that love between two people may be impossible, since each of us lives and dies alone. That state of self-sufficiency is sought most desperately by those who are still filled with humiliating desires for others. Neary, who 'scratches himself from one itch to the next', envies Murphy his freedom from pangs of unrequited love. When asked what it is that women see in Murphy, Wylie says, 'His surgical quality' (39). As the critic Eugene Webb has noted, those who are slaves to emotion secretly worship Murphy for imperviousness to emotional ties.[6]

Even in his attitude to Celia, Murphy is clinical and physical. Celia is a prostitute. She is presented by the narrator with the suggestion that she, all body, may complement Murphy, all mind. But Murphy only wants her for her heavenly body, summed up in the forename Celia (*caeli*, the heavens); and ultimately he wishes to cure himself of his remaining dependency on Celia, gingerbread and so on, so that he can come alive solely in his mind. '"You, my body, my mind",' he tells her, '"one of these will go, or two, or all. If you, then you only; if my body, then you also; if my mind, then all"' (26–7). Seeking pure mind, he has no use for the world of work, but Celia nags him towards salaried employment, if only to free her from her demeaning profession. So they have endless arguments in which she grows inarticulate with rage, with the result that the hyper-literate Murphy has to complete her sentences for her, her very words of anger against himself. The very words which might signal final parting show instead a couple sharing something as intimate as a single sentence.

Nevertheless, in a book of fast and fluent talkers, Celia's hesitations with language betray a greater honesty. Her silences suggest that she may be the most sensitive person of them all, unimpressed by Murphy's glib facility with language:

> She felt, as she felt so often with Murphy, spattered with words that went dead as soon as they sounded; each word obliterated, before it had time to make sense, by the word that came next; so that in the end she did not know what had been said. It was like difficult music heard for the first time. (27)

Celia finds such words to be pure sound devoid of meaning, a version of the MUSIC, MUSIC MUSIC in ascending capitals (132) which they share every night. That capitalised phrase is as near as the Irish censors will permit the narrator go to an account of sexual intercourse, another breakdown of language. But the clearest and most poignant example of that breakdown is Murphy's failure to explain to Celia why he must not go to work. The more he explains, the less she understands. Only when she shares his tranquil silence in the rocking-chair does light begin to dawn on her: 'she began to understand as soon as he gave up trying to explain' (42).

The trouble with this is that it means she must go back to her prostitute's beat, in order to support Murphy in his reveries; and if she must sell her body to other men, then there can be no more music with Murphy. At this argument, Murphy's patience breaks and he asks whether what they feel is love: "'What do you love? […] Me as I am? You can want what does not exist, you can't love it. Then why are you all out to change me? So you won't have to love me?'" (25). He fears, like many men, that his partner wants to change the very thing in him with which she originally fell in love. He fears that what she really loves are her own reasons for loving him, an ideal image of herself as prostitute-turned-respectable-housewife and social reformer. Murphy suspects that her love for him is really an aspect of her love for herself and that what she really esteems is the opportunity he may provide. This is the tragic theme at the heart of every Beckett text – people exist only in their need for one another and use one another as pawns in games of self-love. If Celia worships Murphy for his surgical quality, it is simply in hopes that from him she can learn the art of self-sufficiency, as indeed she does at the end, once she enters the trance made possible by the rocking-chair.

Even when two people share aspirations, Beckett suggests that they can never manage to synchronise them. Celia understands Murphy's need for indolence, but only after her nagging has driven him away. In the last pages, he makes a fleeting resolve to return to Celia, but by then she has achieved self-sufficiency in the chair. In such a world of isolated persons, the idea of desire for another is not only impractical – it is also utterly laughable. And the only way to find peace is to adopt the eastern philosophy of emptying oneself of the desire for created things.

In this context, Murphy must stand convicted of rank hypocrisy, for in the final chapter he violates this moral code on a number of occasions. His last will and testament – indicating that his ashes should be flushed down a toilet at the Abbey Theatre, itself founded to put an end to the Stage Irishman – is in turn a sin, since it involves the act of wishing or desiring something. In fact, it is flagrantly in defiance of his own code, since the will is based on a wish to implement one's desires even after death. It is fitting that this sin should be punished by non-fulfilment, for Murphy's ashes are not in fact scattered down the loo of the Abbey Theatre but rather across the floor of a sawdust pub in London, a place in which the Stage Irishman was often presented as part of a popular entertainment.

Even more serious, however, is the way in which Murphy breaches his own code in his dealings with Mr Endon, an amiable schizophrenic who has already achieved that very self-enclosure of which Murphy still dreams. For Murphy, who has taken work as an orderly at a mental hospital, the psychiatric patients are all heroes who have won the battle for self-sufficiency. What the psychiatrists call exile, he calls sanctuary, and he sees the patients 'not as banished from a system of benefits but as escaped from a colossal fiasco' (101). He tries to learn the secret of self-sufficiency from Mr Endon in a chess-game they play. However, Mr Endon offers no response to Murphy's moves, failing to capture any of Murphy's men, even when Murphy tries his best to lose some. In truth, Mr Endon is entirely unaware of his chess partner. In the end, as Murphy looks into Mr Endon's eye, he sees reflected back just his own image, distorted and reduced on Mr Endon's eyeball.

In other words, Murphy looks hopefully at Mr Endon for some sign of recognition, only to see himself and his own predicament mirrored in Mr Endon's inability to see anything except himself. Just as Celia received only a reduced and distorted image of herself back from Murphy, so now he suffers the same fate at the hands of Mr Endon. To be is, indeed, to be perceived by some other. Moreover, in his approach to Mr Endon, Murphy is guilty of the same hypocrisy of which he had once accused Celia. He had complained that she was guilty of trying to change the very thing in him which she claimed to love, but this is precisely what he is doing to Mr Endon. What he most admires and wishes to emulate is Mr Endon's self-sufficiency; yet it is this self-sufficiency which he seeks to break down in his search for a flicker of recognition from the patient. If Mr Endon had responded, it would have been a catastrophe, for Murphy would have effectively destroyed the one remaining human quality which he claimed to prize above all others.

Murphy's death may be seen in these terms as a fitting punishment for his misdemeanour, and for his failure to appreciate the true situation of the mental patients. Whereas Mr Endon to Murphy was bliss, to Mr Endon he was no more than chess, his eye no more than the 'chessy eye' (135). The opening pages of the book had warned us that Murphy's desire to escape the world of time and contingency was a gross self-deceit. At the start, Murphy sat out of the sun, apart from the measurer of time, 'as though he were free' (5). But he is not at all free of the world: on the second page of the novel that illusion of freedom was described as a fond hope. So, at the end he is shown to have utterly misinterpreted the very real sufferings of the Magdalen Mental Mercyseat patients, not realising that he was 'walking round and round at the foot of the cross' (132) each time he performed his hospital rounds and peered through the Judas hole at the lunatics in their cells. He falsely believed that the patients were having 'a glorious time', but the narrator insists that the narrator had to fight hard to maintain this interpretation against the pressure of actual experience at the hospital: 'Nothing remained but to substantiate these [impressions], distorting all that threatened to belie them. It was strenuous work, but very pleasant' (100).

The deception is finally unmasked. Murphy's trendy modern urge to sentimentalise the deranged as the possessor of higher wisdom is shown to be false. He returns to his own death in the knowledge that, as Virginia Woolf wrote, 'we perish, each alone.' Whether Murphy's death is by suicide or by accident is perhaps of no great account. Some critics point to the fact that Murphy must have resolved to die since he speaks his last words consciously and deliberately as a final utterance:

the last at last seen of him
himself unseen by him
and of himself (140)

Others suggest that, since he decides on a return visit to the flat he shared with Celia at Brewery Road, he has in fact abandoned his illusions about Mr Endon and is ready to return to her. Hence, they claim, the death is a bizarre accident brought on by his absent-mindedness in releasing the gas. It scarcely matters, for by now Celia has lost all interest in the outside world, having perfected the art of coming alive in the mind in her rocking-chair. There is no real need for the narrator to describe her final state of mind, because this has already been done in the account given of Murphy's experience in the rocking-chair in Chapter Six. *This* is, in fact, his real last will – the knowledge of the futility of the workaday world bequeathed at last to the Celia who will take his place.

Like Joyce's *A Portrait of the Artist as a Young Man* this book also offers a tale of a sensitive hero who is left with nobody to talk to but himself. Both books also suggest that the more sensitive a person is, the less likely he is to be able to share that sensitivity with others. Language is a poor, blunt instrument at best and its imperfections would make all honest men and women wince. At the inquest on Murphy, there is a final abuse of language, when a Dr Killiecrankie pronounces Murphy's passing 'A classical case of misadventure' (147). This leads the narrator to make the acid comment: 'words never failed Dr Killiecrankie, that for him would have been tantamount to loose thinking' (147). By a delicious irony, which goes to underwrite Beckett's philosophy that life is a loss of immortality, it turns out that Murphy's remains can be identified only by a birthmark, which thus turns out also to be a death mark.

There are times when the novel almost grinds to a complete halt because of the hyper-sensitive narrator's finicky precision with words and because of his distrust of any word that seems not quite right, which is to say most words. But he persists to the end in telling Murphy's story and that is Beckett's final resting-point. Beckett fully understands the temptation which assails all vulnerable people, to end the unsatisfactory charade of communication with others and lapse into a private world of exquisite sensitivity to the self. That is Murphy's terrible mistake, to think that in the modern world it is enough to defend a private sensibility. But Beckett to his dying day persisted, despite all the odds, in the attempt to communicate something, if only man's sense of loneliness. In fact, he made failure and destitution his major themes. In that, he was a truly Irish author with links right back to those Gaelic bards who, after the collapse of their order in 1600, wrote poems of utter dejection announcing the death of Irish. But they proclaimed this death in lines of such throbbing power as to rebut their very message. They couldn't go on, they said, but went on anyway. Likewise with Beckett. In his writings, all language seems to die, but it records its own demise with such honesty and exactitude as to leave some grounds for hope. Not for nothing did Beckett like to quote a line from Shakespeare's darkest play, *King Lear*: 'The worst is not,/So long as we can say "This is the worst"' (IV.i.25-26). For to be able to describe the collapse of language and culture suggests a mind still able to formulate the sense of cultural crisis: and to be able to formulate suggests, however dimly, the hope of recovery. For these reasons, it would be wrong to call Beckett a nihilist. Long before R.D. Laing and the anti-psychiatrists of the 1960s sought to sentimentalise the mentally ill, Beckett understood that such illness is never enviable and often deeply tragic. He had fought his own way back from depression and learned how to report it with clarity; the findings of that report are chronicled with matchless authority in what may well be his most under-rated book, *Murphy*. It is also one of his funniest books, for as its author was to write twenty years later: 'nothing is funnier than unhappiness'.[7]

J.C.C. MAYS

Beckett as poet: verse, poetry, prose poems

eckett's poems did not earn him the Nobel Prize and, for anyone who has not read anything by Beckett, his poems are definitely not the place to start. At the same time, poems are what he wanted to write at the outset of his career, and he went on writing poems to the end. Also, a good case can be made for thinking that he wrote fiction and drama in a different way from writers whose first ambition was to write novels or plays. The way Beckett wrote in these other forms was determined by his sense of being primarily a poet. He fell into writing novels and plays and they produced, in a paradoxical way, better writing than he had done before: it is as if, after becoming tangled up in what he most wanted to say, he found it easier to address his preoccupations when he established a distance from them. The result is that artistic success is always achieved at the expense of betrayed intentions.

I want to offer comments on three features of Beckett's situation as poet. First, on what you will find if you pick up a collection of his poems in a bookshop or library: say, the latest and most complete collection, *Poems 1930–1989*.[1] If you begin at the beginning, with 'Whoroscope' that won a prize in 1930 and with various uncollected poems written about that time, you will find them strangulated and baffling. Yet it is worth saying something about them because they represent the young Beckett who so impressed Joyce and Jack Yeats and the Parisian avant-garde, as well as his own modernist contemporaries at home. Whatever their limitations, they contain an energy and other qualities that insisted, eventually, on finding an appropriate form. The force of the compulsion can be felt in a little poem that appeared in *The Dublin Magazine*, entitled *Gnome*. It describes the lifelong search for knowledge (*gnosis*) that turns its adherents into withered stumps of humanity (*gnomes*), this description in counterpoint with the spitting energy of the rhymes. The variously placed pauses are a triumph of derision; every run-on line ending rams the truth home harder.

> Spend the years of learning squandering
> Courage for the years of wandering
> Through a world politely turning
> From the loutishness of learning

Secondly, I want to talk about how Beckett wrote himself out of his predicament as a poet by turning from verse to fiction and then to drama, how the different forms allowed him to expand the range of his expression and how, at the same time, his use of them is always hedged about by a sense of their conventions and limitations. To put the matter simply, writing a story about characters, at a distance from the lyric self, supplied his writing with oxygen. Situations opened up from the outside and appeared richer within; authorial distance brought the writing under stricter control. The story of Beckett's relation with fiction is his realisation that conventions have their own necessity: characters need other characters to develop, stories work towards conclusions, authors are steered by plots they invented and are dominated by circumstances they supplied. It keeps happening and there is no escape. The only way to go on is to show how it is; that is, present the dilemma of the writer as the basic fact of life.

Waiting for Godot stages the two novels, *Molloy* and *Malone Dies*; *Endgame* stages the bleaker realisation of the same impasse, *The Unnamable*. So it continues, in play after play, with fewer and fewer words. Beckett turns conventional dramatic form inside out, as he had deconstructed the novel, to provide images of contradiction and self-delusion. One can only say that drama, a group experience, socialises the dilemma: it is searing in a different way from a novel that rips itself apart in a tight writer-reader situation. Besides Beckett's distinctive critical handling of narrative and dramatic form, which I hold to be that of a poet, I want to draw attention to continuing eddies of what can only be called poetry within the larger structures.

My third and last point concerns the development of these poetic eddies into a series of prose poems during Beckett's last great phase of writing. His historically influential poems, the poems and collections that appeared during the 1930s and were admired by Thomas MacGreevy and Brian Coffey, are now at best period pieces.[2] His prose collections following the extended fiction, *How It Is*, comprise prose poems that incorporate the lessons learned in half a lifetime of writing novels and plays, and move on from the vantage gained. Texts like *Imagination Dead Imagine* and *Lessness*, and collections of texts like *Nohow On* and *Stirrings Still*, are poems but not poetry in verse. Beckett's collected *Poems* possess an ancillary interest in relation to the writing that made his reputation. At the same time, his novels and plays are best understood as the work of a poet, as distinct from a convinced novelist or playwright, and they contain moments of wonderful poetry. And then his most achieved poems are not in verse at all. Although he returned to verse towards the end of his days, writing *Mirlitonnades* and *Comment dire* in French (he translated the second only, as *what is the word*), they are only pale shadows of the late prose poems.

I add for those who might think I am stretching a point that the prose poem has an honourable lineage in the language in which Beckett originally wrote his, that is, French. Prose poems are an important part of the oeuvre of Mallarmé, Baudelaire, Valéry and Reverdy; no one would dispute that Rimbaud's prose *Illuminations* contain as much poetry as the rest of his writing. Prose poems are also a viable form in the American tradition: Williams's *Kora in Hell*, Creeley's *Presences* and Ashbery's *Three Poems* possess the status of modern classics.[3] England (and Ireland?) are unusual in their neglect of the genre, which expert opinion suggests may be connected with the tonic stress of the English language, a feature almost completely absent in French and diminished in American English, and the resultant supposition that a poem must be distinguished by some kind of metre. The argument is complicated: in the present instance, the condition of language, French or English, carries the point. Beckett's English publishers categorise his prose poems as shorter fiction, which is what one would expect. The muddled, delayed and still only partial publication of his (verse) poems in France suggests a modest avoidance of the point at issue from the other side.

I can be fairly brief about Beckett's verse *per se*, about which he became increasingly modest. After all, the earlier poems into which he poured his first ambitions overflowed with incoherence, and, when control was established by writing in a medium at a further remove, what went into the poems was only clearer because it was less. The earlier poems that were published in avant-garde magazines are included in a special section at the end of the 2002 collection, with two pages of notes drawn from Beckett's later necessary explications. They are weighed down with allusions and references from extensive reading; they read like pages from *Finnegans Wake* set out in free-verse lines but without Joyce's sense of poetry. The same style continues into the bulk of the collection, *Echo's Bones*, which is arranged around the myth of Narcissus who fell in love with his own reflection in a pool and drowned, while his lover, Echo, wasted away as a result. The myth emblematises the predicament of acute self-consciousness, and the poems evoke the pain. The short title-poem is one of the most successful, mainly because the field of reference is restricted to a well-known resonant source (Prospero in Shakepeare's *Tempest*), and the one unusual word (*gantelope*, an archaic form of 'gauntlet', as in 'running the gantelope/ gauntlet') tells all the more because of its singularity:

> asylum under my tread all this day
> their muffled revels as the flesh falls
> breaking without fear or favour wind
> the gantelope of sense and nonsense run
> taken by the maggots for what they are

Compressed energy jerks through these lines, almost rips up through them in the last line. The same quality distinguishes Beckett's translation of Rimbaud's *Bateau Ivre* (*Drunken Boat*), the most successful of the translations that make up another section of the Calder *Poems*. And this energy, self-contradictory and annihilating when given lyric expression, found more productive forms of expression in fiction and, later, drama. As it did so, Beckett's verse writing became more occasional, more attenuated and more coherent. I mean, it attempted less and, reduced to a peripheral role, achieved more. He began writing directly in French, which increased his control over the inhibiting elements of style that invaded his writing in English. Here is a poem he wrote originally in French and translated himself. It came to him on a visit home, when he was walking on Killiney Strand. It picks up with an image that emerges in the closing pages of his novel *The Unnamable*, which he was working on at that time.

> my way is in the sand flowing
> between the shingle and the dune
> the summer rain rains on my life
> on me my life harrying fleeing
> to its beginning to its end
>
> my peace is there in the receding mist
> when I may cease from treading these long shifting thresholds
> and live the space of a door
> that opens and shuts

This poem is dead simple in its language and evenness of tone, but it contrives a balanced statement of a complicated truth. It communicates a style that mimics Echo's bones more effectively than any of the earlier poems under that title. Conflict is not ended, the gantelope of opposing claims is to be run forever but the solution is balanced on the image of a threshold. If the slightest eloquence is betrayal, if every articulated meaning suppresses the thousand possibilities of development from which it emerged, this kind of imaged truth, communicated in a style which denies every aid of solidified statement, is the way forward. This is as good as it gets in Beckett's book of *Poems*, all he could manage and more than he could in verse. I want to turn next, as promised, to eddies of poetry in his contemporary novels and plays.

Beckett's writing in extended forms – novels and plays – is episodic. That is, it advances by a sequence of discrete episodes, which tend to wind themselves up with increasing speed until the mood flips and they go into reverse. One of his characters explains:

> I could no more do [the jog trot] than I could fly. No, with me all was slow, and then these flashes, or gushes, vent the pent, that was one of the things I used to say, over and over, as I went along, vent the pent, vent the pent.[4]

This is what I want to talk about under my second heading – examples of these 'flashes, or gushes,' what I called eddies, that are produced by the vent-the-pent, alternating impulses of the prose. I'll take an example from the selection Beckett chose for Jack MacGowran. It may be familiar to some of you from the gramophone/CD recording *Beginning to End*, or you may have seen Barry McGovern speaking the same passages from the stage.

So, take the set-piece passage from the novel *Watt*, the second item in the MacGowran recording,[5] the one beginning 'The Tuesday scowls, the Wednesday growls, the Thursday curses, the Friday howls, the Saturday snores, the Sunday yawns, the Monday morns, the Monday morns.' Notice how the words rhyme in a lopsided way, until the minimal pattern (AABA, CDDD) is buried by monotony. The possibility of rhyme is thereupon taken up with more determination, alternating stimulus and response – 'The whacks the moans, the cracks, the groans,' and so on – and the rhymes turn out to mimic the elaborate pattern of a Shakespearean sonnet (ABAB, CDCD, EFEF, GG) with its couplet-closure ('the skelps, and the yelps'). This time, conscious effort is buried by convention. Finally, returning wearily to beginnings, you shift into a parody of biblical genealogy: 'my father's father's and my mother's mother's and my father's mother's' and so on, continually rounding to a balance but then building further, until purpose is overtaken by articulation and your mind glazes over. 'An excrement.'

At this point, the paragraph shifts into a higher gear, the formulaic repetition is replaced by suspended syntax and present participles, the staccato rhythm is smoothed out with linking 'ands' and repeated phrases – 'and the smell of the gorse and the look of the gorse and the apples falling and the children walking in the dead leaves' – until this idyll is in turn undercut by the consumptive postman whistling a First World War tune 'and then the whole bloody business starting all over again. A turd.' The prose is written with as much care as poetry, and the paragraph is organised to proceed with as much care as a poem. The two phases I have described are equivalent to stanzas, and they are completed by a third in which the tempo shifts again, and darker chords are struck. In this concluding phase the tense is repeatedly conditional. 'And if I could begin it all over again a hundred times, knowing each time a little more than the time before, knowing what I know now, the result would always be the same, and the hundredth life as the first, and the hundred lives as one. A cat's flux.'

The set-piece passage rewrites the poem *Echo's Bones* ('asylum under my tread'), but the transposition into prose enables a much wider variety of effect. It begins with the rehearsal of traditional formulae, out of which, as they replace one another and yet come to repeat one another, maniacal self-destructive energy emerges. The focus shifts to a surrounding, comforting world that follows the same process of disintegration, becomes stuck in the mire of sentiment. And, finally, the close of the passage, that reflects on this circular entrapment – 'the gantelope of sense and nonsense run' – makes up, as it combines with the previous phases of the statement, a particularly rich conclusion. Not just bitter or resigned – 'taken for the maggots for what they are' – but with sentiment and hilarity, too. This is what I mean by saying that Beckett's turn to prose gave his poetry wider scope. What was confused or constricted opened out and was reincorporated on the writer's terms.

Other examples could be given from other novels: for instance, the sucking-stones episode from *Molloy*[6] that MacGowran and McGovern have both performed with aplomb. The episode winds through different phases like the passage from *Watt*, although the phases themselves are different. Molloy first attempts a method of sucking stones in *regular succession*. It promises an intellectual satisfaction so intense as to fulfil an almost bodily need, and of course expectations wind up to a pitch where they can only fail. So he attempts a different method, sucking stones according to a scheme of *equal distribution*, which addresses bodily need but fails to satisfy intellectually. The set piece is organised to present the same sense of aporia as before, but differently within a different emotional context. The same sense of maniacal absorption is communicated, hilarity evaporating above an abyss, but it is compressed within a tighter framework of choice, both the intellectual and the practical solutions failing.

As an example from a play, take the well-known piece of dialogue between Estragon and Vladimir in *Waiting for Godot* beginning, 'All the dead voices.'[7] It appeared in Derek Mahon's *Sphere Book of Modern Irish Poetry* (1972) as a poem under that title, and so of course it is, although it is in prose. It advances through five phases, separated by the stage direction '*Silence*', each phase a stanza. Estragon's voice is the constant: it opens and closes the first stanza. Vladimir's voice begins each stanza thereafter, with Estragon bringing each stanza to rest and having the final word. The antiphonal rhythm sets up a tension between stasis and movement, acceptance and change. A statement is made in stanza 1:

ESTRAGON: All the dead voices.
VLADIMIR: They make a noise like wings.
ESTRAGON: Like leaves.
VLADIMIR: Like sand.
ESTRAGON: Like leaves.

In stanza 2, the opposition stanza 1 contains is given a more symmetrical shape and concentrated:

VLADIMIR: They all speak together.
ESTRAGON: Each one to itself.

From this, an enlarged statement grows in stanza 3:

VLADIMIR: Rather they whisper.
ESTRAGON: They rustle.
VLADIMIR: They murmur.
ESTRAGON: They rustle.

The statement grows further again in stanza 4 as Vladimir insists on entertaining hope:

VLADIMIR: What do they say?
ESTRAGON: They talk about their lives.
VLADIMIR: To have lived is not enough for them.
ESTRAGON. They have to talk about it.
VLADIMIR: To be dead is not enough for them
ESTRAGON: It is not sufficient.

And then, in stanza 5, having been so buoyed up, there is no way but down. Vladimir's wings become feathers, his sand becomes ashes, and Estragon's vision of dead leaves prevails:

VLADIMIR: They make a noise like feathers.
ESTRAGON: Like leaves.
VLADIMIR: Like ashes.
ESTRAGON: Like leaves.

The evident patterning creates a verbal ballet that epitomises the larger themes and the more extreme emotions of the play as a whole.

My comments treat the passage as a piece of writing to be read, but the theatrical context reminds us it was conceived to be read or heard differently from the way a poem or novel is read. We engage with the spectacle of Estragon and Vladimir from the position of an audience, across footlights; we engage with real actors 'as if' they were the characters in the play, sitting alongside others, the audience of which we form a part. In the picture-frame situation Beckett's plays normally specify, the particular kind of illusion supposes a degree of formal estrangement, and his writing for the stage is always more shapely and balanced. At the same time, the issues presented, while they are the same as in the novels and poetry, are more often the subject of humour or sentiment. The stage is welcomed as a means of demonstration, and is not, like fiction, used as a means of solution. Fallen leaves are an enduring simile for the numberless dead: the trope appears in Isaiah, Homer, Virgil, Dante and Milton, among others. In the passage from *Watt*, the postman's whistled tune recalling fallen companions who lie in Picardy is contained by this same tradition. In *Godot*, the allusion is overtaken by a physical image of two men, one fat with smelly feet and the other thin with smelly breath. The dialogue merely suffuses the spectacle: the gulf between the two men is more than an intellectual option. It is real – they are simply not the same – and their words echo across that sad, terrifying gulf.

I have left little time to discuss my third topic, Beckett's prose poems, which is as well because his later writing is the subject of a later lecture in this series. If one can accept the un-English notion that such a literary category exists, Beckett's later texts must be counted as the culmination of his writing as a poet. The glory is that there are so many of them: besides those already named, one could add *From an Abandoned Work, Ping,*

As the Story Was Told, Company and a dozen more. It is no accident that they have attracted numerous illustrators, indeed, that some of them first appeared as collaborative enterprises: they are intensely visual. They describe situations on which to meditate: the journeying of the novels is over. Nor is it an accident that several of them that exist in both French and English evolved symbiotically, each influencing the composition of the other, neither original and neither completive. They exist in a literally in-between state, suspended between their alternative actualisations. The mingling of voices and merging of layers of self is extraordinarily rich. We engage with them as poetry, not as fiction or drama, however much they owe to experiments with those forms. They seem to me the completion of his career as a poet: 'what is the word', *Comment dire*.

There is only one thing to add: Beckett came increasingly to believe that his purpose as a dramatist was to set an image resonating in the mind. The dramatic experience of such texts works in the exactly same way as a visual poem by Robert Lax or Ian Hamilton Finlay: three talking heads locked in hellish repetition, an old woman walking up and down or rocking in a chair, a devouring mouth voiding sound. His later fictional texts or prose poems, too, celebrate still moments that ripple like a clear spring fed from beneath: the surrounding words fall away in importance. On occasion, such as in *Quad*, the only words remaining are stage directions. Poetry has moved not only beyond verse but beyond words.

ANTHONY ROCHE

samuel beckett: the great plays after godot

Shortly after Samuel Beckett won the Nobel Prize for literature in late October 1969, I watched a programme on his work on British television which concentrated on the UK première of his latest play, *Breath*. The entire performance consisted of the light coming up on a stage 'littered with miscellaneous rubbish',[1] a brief cry, a heightening and lowering of the light to a minimum, an identical brief cry (both were recorded) and after a pause of five seconds, the final curtain. In the TV programme, this was followed by a brace of commentary from various experts, the chief of whom argued that while at first glance *Breath* might not appear to have much to offer, it acquired meaning with each subsequent re-viewing until, the twentieth time around, you saw God. Beckett and his work would instantly have been filed under the category of 'Pseud's Corner' were it not for the fact that in the same month this eighteen-year-old had experienced one of his greatest ever nights at the theatre (then or since) when he saw the Abbey Theatre production of *Waiting for Godot* with Peter O'Toole as Vladimir, Donal McCann as Estragon and Eamon Kelly as

Pozzo. It was profound, moving and funny. When I came to study *Godot* formally, first at his alma mater Trinity College, Dublin, and subsequently in the US with that great Beckettian Vivian Mercier, I realised the extent to which *Godot's* first performance in Paris in January 1953 had effected what amounted to a Copernican revolution in world theatre. Its minimalist approach to drama and its combination of high philosophical discussion with broad physical farce gave the play its inimitable flavour. *Waiting for Godot* was rapidly acclaimed, translated into English and has played ever since to audiences around the world – an avant-garde work which proved enduringly popular. A great play, indisputably. Of how many more of the plays Beckett subsequently offered for production, numbering eighteen in all, could this be said? I have chosen to concentrate on four which seem to me to merit the term 'great', offering as they do a perfect fusion of form and content, theatrical experiments which work not at the expense but to the realisation of what it means to be fully human.

The first of these is *Godot's* successor, *Endgame*. What is so striking about it in terms of Beckett's previous play is the extent to which its author has been exposed to the medium of the theatrical act in the meantime. In *Endgame* Beckett submits to the formal demands of theatre and his characters are compelled to do no less. Where a great deal of theatrical freedom was extended to the characters in *Eleutheria* and the two principals of *Godot* when it came to movement, gestures and so on, the stage directions of *Endgame* are so numerous, precise and detailed as to amount to an act of choreography. In the elaborate wordless mime with which the play commences, Clov's movements back and forth between the two windows is measured out in terms of the precise number of steps he takes. The setting is no longer the outside world of *Godot* with its emblems of the natural world, the tree and the stone. *Endgame* has turned resolutely against nature and moved into a bare interior, artificially illuminated, where the degree and kind of light can be precisely regulated. This is also an open space of possibility, the bare stage of the thousands of years of enacted theatre. Since it is bare, all of the objects required have to be either onstage already – Hamm's chair, the two ashcans – or have to be brought on by Clov in his role as stage manager: the ladder, the telescope, the alarm clock. All of them are artificial, man-made objects whose formal and theatrical properties are presented to us self-consciously by Clov: 'I'm back again, with the glass' (105). As will be the case with Winnie, these objects are props in not only a theatrical but a psychological sense, aids to preserve a semblance of identity and to help keep the show on the road.

There is very little initially to grasp at in the way of psychological depth in terms of the individual characters. The play instead seems to suggest we look at the relationships between them. Hamm and Clov enjoy or at least endure a master–servant relationship similar to that between Pozzo and Lucky in *Godot* but now promoted from the margins to centre-stage. The insistent theatricalisation encourages us to view them as director/author and actor/manager. Certainly, Hamm gives all of the orders in terms of how the stage space is set, arranged and occupied. And he spends a portion of the time self-consciously getting on with writing his 'chronicle', as he calls it: a Dickensian narrative of a poor man with tears streaming down his grimy face begging a rich man (Hamm) to give bread to his starving child. Hamm wishes to be the centre of creation, insisting he is placed at the centre of the room. His pose of absolute power and independence is crucially undermined in a number of ways, however. This is the more evident when the play is seen as well as read, given that Hamm's assertions of power are verbal. But he lacks physical independence. Unable to move, he remains in his chair throughout and has to be physically moved from place to place by Clov, his 'legs'. Even more seriously, he cannot see and so depends on Clov for his visual record of the world and for its interpretation. When the artificial black dog is brought on and Hamm asks, 'He's white, isn't he?' Clov replies, 'Nearly' (111). Hamm also has to depend absolutely on Clov for information on what exists outside their bunker, in the elaborate business by which Clov mounts the ladder to the two windows and trains the telescope on the outside. In response to Hamm's insistent questioning, Clov replies with the neutral tones of 'Nothing' or 'grey' (107). Like the author in the theatre, Hamm may wish to assert his royal prerogatives but is fatally dependent on the services of others for the staging of the play and (it is suggested) its ultimate meaning.

But if Hamm and Clov collectively stage *Endgame*, there are two other character-actors so far unaccounted for. Nagg and Nell do not come onstage. Rather, they unexpectedly emerge from the ashcans we have seen from the beginning and announce their presence. Hamm does not want them around and cannot endure their presence for long before insisting they are 'bottled'. But they are necessary to him in a double sense. For Hamm's story requires an audience if it is to achieve its full authenticity and in this case the reluctant audience has to be bribed to listen with sugarplums. Nagg in turn insists that Nell be an audience to his oft-told story of the tailor who makes the pair of trousers, because it always made her laugh. Like father, like son. For that is the crux on which the story of the play turns. Nagg and Nell are Hamm's parents, and at one level the image of their being confined to ashcans provides an apt metaphor of how older people are treated in the late twentieth century. But their emergence from the ashcans, particularly at moments when Hamm is engaging in a reverie, also suggests that they are constant presences in his subconscious, voices which he cannot keep entirely silent or under, however much he may prefer to. As has often been remarked, the set of *Endgame* suggests that we are inside a human skull, with the two windows as eyes or apertures, etc., and that the characters are various components of a single psyche.[2]

As always in Beckett, the characters' physical inter-dependence suggests that they are no less psychologically interknit. *Endgame*, therefore, is a play about family, something that marks it off from *Godot*, where the characters have a shared history but no blood ties. What of the relation between Hamm and Clov? The narrative about the rich man being encouraged to adopt the starving boy is designed to suggest that Clov is the latter and that he has been adopted by Hamm. As he says: 'It was I was a father to you' (110). In his opening monologue, Hamm has spoken of his father and his mother. Towards the end, he refers to his father and his son. He stumbles over the latter, which may suggest that 'son' is the best way he can find to identify Clov, but also that he has difficulty in acknowledging him as his own blood. Throughout the play, Hamm manifests a constant fear that humanity will start all over again, whether from a flea, a rat or the young boy whom Clov claims to discern on the horizon. As he sits on his throne, King Hamm wants all lineage to culminate in him and to leave no issue, to acknowledge no successor. But he is the man in the middle, caught between the parents he seeks to deny but cannot, and the son whom emotionally he cannot admit but is forced to rely upon for more and more of his being in the world. Clov argues that he will leave him but even at the end, when he is comically *dressed for the road [in his] panama hat, tweed coat, raincoat over his arm, umbrella, bag* (132), he is unable to leave. The 'endgame' of the play is finally that of family relations, which persist even as they are insistently denied.

In *Endgame* Beckett had gone to dramatic and linguistic extremes, writing a second play in French which he found it extremely difficult to translate into English. *Krapp's Last Tape* by contrast was written first in his mother tongue, English, before he translated it into French and has been recognised as one of his most autobiographical works. Indeed, the death of Beckett's own mother is installed at the heart of the play's central monologue: 'there is of course the house on the canal where mother lay a-dying, in the late autumn' (219). The immediate inspiration for Beckett had been the sound of the Irish actor Patrick Magee's *'cracked voice [with] distinctive intonation'* (215) which he had heard reciting Beckett's prose on a BBC Radio Three programme.[3] Another Irish voice leaves its traces in the play: old Miss McGlome, who is from Connaught, has earlier that night been singing a hymn which Krapp continues to sing in the course of the play. Its central character is, like Beckett, a writer, one who has dedicated his life to writing but who has had spectacularly little success, as the dismal sales of his slim volume of poetry reveal. The forms of writing discussed by Krapp are the poems and the *magnum opus*, which is presumably a work in prose; but Krapp's methods of composition in the play, which are presented directly to us, show a mode of dramatic experimentation. Beckett's own writing in both prose and poetry only rose to prominence in the aftermath of *Godot's* success, about which he couldn't help but be ambivalent.

Beckett has formalised and distanced these personal elements of *Krapp's Last Tape* in a number of important ways. He stages a complex self-encounter through the inspired use of a tape-recorder. And he also projects the events into '*the future*' (215), so that Krapp is celebrating his seventieth birthday, whereas Beckett was only in his early fifties when he wrote the play. What I wish to stress in the play with the tape-recorder is what it both enables and requires of the actor playing Krapp. Because what we are presented with through this device is virtually two different people: the confident, rather pompous thirty-nine-year-old, convinced he is at the height of his creative powers; and the more weary, regretful seventy-year-old who retains his taste for bananas and whose relish is now more for the sounds of words rather than their meaning: 'Spooool!' (216). In *Philadelphia, Here I Come!* Brian Friel had two actors play the divided young protagonist, Gar O'Donnell. Here, Beckett has the one actor play the two divided sides of Krapp through the medium of voice. But the seventy-year-old Krapp himself has more than one voice: the voice of the father who bursts out with 'Jesus! Take his mind off his homework!' (222) and the voice of the mother, whose presence is registered through the play's more lyrical tone and its recurrent focusing on a number of women. As Beckett himself put it: 'A woman's tone goes through the entire play.'[4]

The most recent, and one of the most memorable, Krapps has been John Hurt, whose craggy features and springy hair visually resembled the author's. He played the part both in the

Beckett on Film project and in the Gate Theatre performance in September 2001. I had agreed to review this production for Myles Dungan on RTÉ Radio One's arts programme, *Rattlebag*, on a date which suited us both: 11 September 2001. I walked down from UCD on a mild, sunny autumn day and when I arrived at the RTÉ studios entered a scene of absolute chaos: people running up and down corridors, babbling the shocking news that a plane had gone into the Twin Towers building in New York and that nobody quite knew what was going to happen next. As I waited to go on, the three o'clock news revealed that a second plane had crashed into the skyscraper. At 3.30 p.m. the details of 9/11 were to take over the airwaves. In the meantime, Myles and I had to review Beckett's play. I tried to keep my focus even as my mind grappled with what the possible loss of life might be. In retrospect, I was very glad the programme was going out live because, although we never explicitly referred to what was going on in New York, it simultaneously informed everything we said. Myles's final question asked whether the play might not as well be on radio, whether it was sufficiently dramatic. I stressed the importance of the onstage Krapp as a live presence, listening to something unalterable on a recorded medium, which he can fast forward, rewind and replay, but which has already, irrevocably happened: in this case, the tragedy of missed opportunities which is his life. The older Krapp is not only an actor; he's a member of the audience, listening to this recording and adding his own comment to it. The play dramatises the insufficiency of language, its inability to convey the profoundest emotion. The play's true drama resides in Krapp's act of listening, his reactions to what he is hearing: the raising of an eyebrow, a profound look of sadness at its inevitability. The following week, an Irish publication protested that as 9/11 unfolded, RTÉ radio was broadcasting a review of Beckett's *Krapp's Last Tape*; no doubt he had us lined up for 'Pseud's Corner'. Perhaps. But there are and were worse things to be doing as an apocalyptic event unfolded. What struck me forcibly was the greatness of Beckett's play in being adequate to the awfulness of the historic moment, its ongoing prophetic ability to address world events long after its composition.

Winnie in *Happy Days* is the first major woman's part in any of Beckett's stage plays and has been memorably played by a variety of great actresses over the years, from Marie Kean to Rosaleen Linehan. This lecture has traced the emergence of women onto the hitherto all-male Beckettian stage, first with the brief emergence of Nell from her ashcan in *Endgame*, then with the presence of Beckett's mother in *Krapp's Last Tape*. What occurs in *Happy Days* is in gender terms a Copernican revolution to match that of *Godot's* radical dramaturgy. Not only does it feature a woman in a major part but it promotes the woman to centre stage, at the exact centre of a mound which like all of the stage's sloping contours has a feminine shape. The actress playing Winnie never enjoys freedom of movement. She is buried to her waist in the first act, with very restricted movement, and to her neck in the second, with no movement at all. What she does get to do is to speak, and the two-act play is virtually a monologue, a tour-de-force of Winnie keeping the words going so that she can get through her day and so that we have a play to attend to.

And where is the male in all of this? Willie, her husband, is on the far side of the mound, physically unencumbered but barred from the viewing of the audience except on the rare occasions when his head or hand comes into view. And what does Willie do with his greater freedom? He spends the day sleeping or sitting in the sun, picking his nose, moving in and out of a hole in the sand dune, reading notices and ads from a yellowed newspaper or inspecting a pornographic postcard. Occasionally, when she begs to be acknowledged, he throws his wife a scrap of conversation, rarely more than several syllables and a repetition of what she has just said. It is often claimed that *Waiting for Godot* and *Endgame* are portraits of a marriage, of two people who have operated together as a couple for decades, filling their lives with routine, endlessly rowing and threatening to part but never summoning up the energy or nerve to do so. But these are all-male couples, a fact to which Beckett criticism has all along turned a blind eye. Willie and Winnie *are* a married couple, in social as well as dramatic reality, well epitomised by Winnie's account of what married life to Willie has been like: 'I worship you Winnie be mine and then nothing from that day forth only titbits from *Reynolds' News*' (167).

Beckett has as it were turned the conventional stage on its axis. Where the wife traditionally stood behind the husband who went forth into the public world, Winnie has been promoted to the foreground of the stage, so that she is the one the audience sees, listens to and engages with, while Willie is relegated to the background. Any recognisable social reality is held at bay by the surrealistic setting and context of the play. Winnie and Willie are not in a realistic suburban household but stranded in a wilderness, an '*expanse of scorched grass rising centre to a low mound*' (138). They are there without explanation, and Winnie (as has been said) is buried up to the waist. The artificiality of the stage setting is enhanced by the backcloth which represents '*unbroken plain and sky receding to meet in far distance*' (138). In this alien and defamiliarising setting Winnie goes through her day. A considerable aid to her is the handbag containing a variety of objects which are produced and used: the brush to comb her hair, the mirror to inspect her features, the toothbrush whose writing she spends most of the play trying to read and decipher, the lipstick which she applies. In this context, they are as much theatrical as female props, aids to the rituals of behaviour which inform and structure her waking moments.

The rituals of *Happy Days* are as much verbal as visual. Never has a Beckett text been more attuned to the niceties of cliché, to the turns of phrase which litter everyday conversation. Winnie talks repeatedly of wanting this day to be another 'happy day'. But she has to admit she's employing the 'old style' in her locutions, since night and day no longer exist in this blasted landscape. Some of the verbal formulae which help her are poems and plays from the classic repertoire of English literature, which she has committed to memory at an early stage and which exist now as half-recalled fragments. Winnie begins her day at the start of Act One with thanks for 'another heavenly day' (138) and two silently murmured prayers which culminate with a spoken formula: 'For Jesus Christ sake Amen' and 'World without end, Amen' (138). At the end of the act, she is unable to say her prayer, despite her best efforts to do so. None of these cultural texts is presented with any formal precision or authority – they are half-remembered, at best, are summoned to satisfy a psychic need in their speaker rather than for any formal occasion. But in a very real sense Winnie does not need them. They are the residues of a patriarchal authority which may once have held meaning and solace but which now are fading from cultural memory. The words which most characterise and sustain Winnie are those she generates herself, none of which is funnier or more critically trenchant than the husband and wife she conjures up to comment on the spectacle that the play presents of a woman buried to her waist in sand. The husband combines the baffled query of the critic – 'What's it meant to mean?' (156) – with the sexual prurience of the voyeur: 'Has she anything on underneath?' (165). His questions are turned on him by his wife: 'And you, she says, what's the idea of you, she says, what are you meant to mean?' (156).

The last of the four Beckett plays I wish briefly to consider is *Come and Go*, which received its world première in English at the newly opened Peacock Theatre in Dublin in 1968. It has an all-female cast of three: Flo, Vi and Ru, who wear full-length coats of the appropriate colour (yellow, red and violet) and sit together on a bench facing the audience. Their ages are (as Beckett specifies) 'undeterminable' (353) but an entire lifetime is conjured up and ecapsulated in Flo's line: 'Just sit together as we used to, in the playground at Miss Wade's' (354). The play's action consists of a pattern of movement with one of the three moving off while the other two whisper about some unnamed ailment from which their friend is suffering and of which they hope she is unaware. At the close they join hands in an elaborate pattern which visually suggests a Celtic design and beautifully symbolises the patterns of involvement and affection, of sisterhood, which have bound the three women together all their lives. The opening line, Vi's 'When did we three last meet?' (354), deliberately recalls even as it revises the famous opening line of Shakespeare's Scottish play: 'When shall we three meet again?'[5] The witches in *Macbeth* have to give way to not only the title character but to the patriarchal tussling over who will secure the Scottish crown for the future. The women in *Come and Go* remain at the centre of their play and remain undemonised. Their names, especially Ru's, recall the names of the flowers which Ophelia distributes to King Claudius and his court in her mad scene. But Flo, Vi and Ru do not have to run mad to gain a measure of dramatic freedom and centrality. Women occupied the key roles in Shakespeare's comedies. *Come and Go* is a tragedy, in which the women have spent time 'dreaming of ... love' (355) and in which each has contracted a fatal ailment. But they assert a strength through their interdependence which makes of this play one of the most perfect theatrical ensembles ever devised.

The next play after *Come and Go* in Beckett's *Complete Dramatic Works* is *Breath*, with which we began. Thankfully, this latter was not the last gasp in his dramatic output, as it threatened to be. In 1972, the complex and fascinating *Not I* was premièred; and there were to be seven more stage plays. Each of them has its interest; and there are several of them I love, as I suspect is the case with most Beckettians. But these later plays seem like variants, verbal and technical elaborations, on what the great plays have already established: the head of Winnie is further reduced to the Mouth of *Not I*; the male solitaries of the last plays come and go from their refuges and sanctums but bearing a lesser human and dramatic freight than Krapp. There were to be noteable Beckett plays after *Breath*, but without the amplitude and (dare I say it?) breadth of what had preceded, even in the two pages of *Come and Go*.

ROSEMARY
POUNTNEY

stringent demands: aspects of Beckett in performance

T he performance of Beckett's shorter plays for the theatre makes exceptional demands on the actor, audience, technicians and director alike. This lecture will discuss the stringency of Beckett's requirements in these areas and consider to what extent the exacting nature of such demands may present problems for the continuing life of the plays, both today and in the future.

To begin with the actor: Jack MacGowran described the television camera narrowing steadily in on his face in *Eh Joe* exposing his haunted eyes as 'the most gruelling twenty-two minutes I have ever had in my life'[1], and Brenda Bruce described 'Beckett placing a metronome on the floor to keep me on the rhythm he wanted, which drove me into such a panic that I finally broke down'.[2] Billie Whitelaw similarly remarked that, when rehearsing *Not I*, Beckett told her that she had 'paused for two dots instead of three'.[3] Whitelaw also describes in her autobiography losing self-confidence un-expectedly when rehearsing *Happy Days* with Beckett and asking advice from Dame Peggy Ashcroft, who said: 'He's impossible. Throw him out.'[4] Dame Peggy herself appeared uncomfortable in her early performances as Winnie (at the Old Vic in 1974) though she had grown into the role by the time *Happy Days* transferred to the Lyttelton in 1976, as the National Theatre's opening production.[5] Albert Finney too appeared uneasy in *Krapp's Last Tape* in 1973, lacking his usual mastery of a role.[6] Contemplating such uncharacteristic discomfort from both actors one wondered whether, in trying to achieve what Beckett wanted, they had found themselves acting against their own theatrical instincts and had thus not fully integrated into their roles.

Nonetheless many actors develop an extraordinary rapport with their roles when performing Beckett, an identification at an unusually profound level, resulting in a catharsis of equal depth. The very fact that Beckett denies them so much of their normal means of expression in the theatre seems to act as a stimulus, a challenge to creativity. They may be restricted in movement (trapped in urns or in mid-air itself, with their voices reduced to a monotone 'as low as compatible with audibility' or to speech so fast that it can hardly be registered by an audience; even to becoming mere listeners to their own recorded voices[7] or to speechless virtual automatons, as in *Quad*) but such deprivation forces actors to dig deeper into themselves than is the norm in the theatre. As it is not possible to build up a character in the usual way (when playing an old woman, for example, part of the process would normally involve close observation of how such women move and speak) in *Not I* there is no movement about the stage, no opportunity for facial expression, just the mouth pouring out words at great speed, preventing even much variation of pace.

The actress is thus forced to go beyond the norms of performance. Rather than a process of accretion, of building *up* a character, she must try to strip her performance *down* to the inner core, creating an interior space, an emptiness, denuded of self, yet actively alert to the Beckett text. In effect she becomes a receptacle for the text and it is the challenge of going beyond the normal boundaries of performance that produces the depth of identification with the role that actors find so exhilarating and brings about their close rapport with Beckett.

It is with the performance of Beckett's plays for women that I am principally concerned. The earliest plays (*Godot* being the obvious example) are notable for the absence of women. Mme Piouk and Mme Krap in *Eleutheria* are clearly in the realm of caricature, while Nell in *Endgame* is outnumbered by three to one and apparently expires during the performance, ceding the stage to the male. It is in *Happy Days* that Beckett, having experimented successfully with monologue in *Krapp's Last Tape,* introduces a female monologue, broken only by the rare interruptions (so avidly courted by Winnie) from her exiguous husband. Madeleine Renaud, who played Winnie in the first French production,[8] remarked on the depth of Beckett's understanding of women. It is in *Happy Days* that the sardonic, generally grotesque portrayals of women from the prose and early plays give place in Winnie to a distinct personality, in a searing account of marriage from both the female and the male perspectives.

After *Happy Days*, which is at least recognisably concerned with *terra firma*, Beckett's plays become shorter and increasingly experimental, tending to move towards limbo in terms of staging. Performing the short plays for women is, as already indicated, hugely demanding. Billie Whitelaw, when rehearsing *Not I* for the first London production,[9] her head enclosed in a Ku Klux Klan-type hood, developed such a sense of disorientation that, as described by Brian Miller, who played the Auditor,[10] she had to stop. A different method was therefore devised in which she sat, face blacked out, in a dentist's chair, her head positioned so that the narrow lightbeam would illuminate her mouth alone. After a time, however, it became possible for audiences of this production to distinguish black from black, so that the faint outline of a solid figure behind the mouth became apparent in the surrounding darkness.

In order to prevent this happening again for the play's second English production (at Oxford Playhouse in 1976) a radical solution was proposed by the lighting director.[11] A blackout curtain was let down upstage, covering the entire stage area. The actress was placed on a scaffold just behind the curtain, positioned so that her mouth was the precise eight feet above stage level prescribed by Beckett. At this point a hole was cut in the curtain at mouth level, so that her mouth could protrude through the curtain. In order that the image should remain constant, however, and not move in and out of the hole when taking a breath, the most fiendish part of the procedure was devised. A piece of elasticated material with strings attached was sewn to the inside of the curtain, surrounding the hole. Into this the actress was tied before the start of the performance. (Having been that actress I recall with feeling the extreme sense of isolation experienced on hearing the assistant stage manager's footsteps retreating down the scaffolding after tying me in!) Discussing this with Beckett some time later, he described the play as 'a horror' for the actress.[12]

It is evident that the technical input is crucial when performing Beckett's shorter female roles. Much of the action is initiated by lighting and recorded sound interacting with the performer, who therefore relies on the skills of the technical staff to a much greater extent than is usual in the theatre. The synchronisation of light, sound and silence must operate in precise conjunction with the performer, which requires great sensitivity of technical direction. Indeed the performance may stand or fall on the seamless integration of the technical effects. To begin with stage lighting, *Play* is an obvious example, since all utterance from the three urns is controlled by light, which becomes in effect a fourth character. When all three heads are illuminated, they speak as a chorus; if a single head is isolated, that actor speaks alone. In *Krapp's Last Tape* and *Come and Go* deep surrounding darkness is eerily emphasised by only the centre of the stage being lit. In these shadows (as Beckett once remarked) 'old Nick' awaits Krapp[13] and the fate of Flo, Vi and Ru appears to be similar. In *Not I* and *That Time* the protagonist is partially illuminated, suspended in a limbo of darkness; in *Footfalls* May literally walks up and down a strip of light on the stage floor that dims from scene to scene, but remains vestigially present at the end of the play, thus registering her absence. In *Rockaby* light also dims from scene to scene, finally revealing W's head falling slowly to rest, after the rocking chair has 'rock(ed) her off'.

In terms of sound, Beckett's revolutionary use of the actor's voice has been noted; its tonal reduction to a monotone or paced to a gallop in *Not I*, where the voice is literally torn from the mouth like the scream of pain it utters at one stage. It is with the use of the recorded voice that the actor's reliance on technical support becomes total. In *Rockaby*, for example, most of the play is spent with W listening to her recorded voice, until the end of each scene, where she joins in with the recording to repeat the concluding phrase. Initial rehearsals must therefore begin with a recording being made and it is advisable at this stage simply to make a workable tape, which can be improved on at a later date, after the performance has been developed.

Several of Beckett's short plays operate on diminishing effects between scenes. The technique is first used in *Play* where both light and voice levels are reduced after the first scene, following a blackout, but are restored to their original state when the play is repeated. 'Exact repeat preferable' Beckett wrote when I enquired about this, since, in a Paris production, he had once experimented with light dwindling further in the repeat, towards a possible extinction.[14] In *Footfalls* and *Rockaby* a gradual diminuendo is allowed to develop throughout both plays. In *Footfalls* Beckett worked with the idea of diminution on several levels. At the beginning of the play the light is already 'dim' and the single chime 'faint' and both are reduced further at each blackout between scenes. The actors' voices remain 'low and slow' throughout, but the number of lengths paced by May and the speed at which she does so reduces between scenes and her body becomes more hunched over as her energy fails. Discussing this with me, Beckett pointed out that on her last walk along the strip of light, her energy runs out after three paces and she has to wait there until enough vitality returns to drag herself to the end of the light.[15] This clearly links with the final scene, where the very faintest light and chime reveal an empty stage, with 'No trace of May.'

In *Rockaby* the light level is reduced after every scene, though a subdued spotlight on W's face remains 'constant throughout'. The recorded voice also remains constant until the last twelve lines, where it softens to a whisper; but W's request to hear 'More' of the recording does lessen from scene to scene. In both these plays Beckett makes technical use of echo effects. In *Footfalls* the echoes of the single chime herald the start of every scene, reducing each time until the very shadow of a chime sounds at the end of the play. In *Rockaby* the final lines of every scene are echoed, so that, as the play ends, the last sibilant whispered line 'rock her off' echoes around the theatre. In *Rockaby* also Beckett gives an extraordinarily daring stage direction, challenging for both actor and audience, regarding the opening and closing of the protagonist's eyes. Beckett had first tried this out in *That Time*, where the brief opening of Listener's eyes between scenes registers his extreme interest in the silence, the cessation of the three voices that assail him in each scene. In *Rockaby* Scene One, W's eyes are either 'open in unblinking gaze' or closed 'in about equal proportions', but become increasingly closed in Scenes Two and Three until, half-way through the final scene, they are (as Beckett tersely notes) 'closed for good'.

There is of course no way of covering up a technical hitch in minimalist drama. Performing *Rockaby* in French in Strasbourg, for instance, the sound level of the recorded tape had been set too high in error and there was nothing to be done but sit in the rocking chair and suffer![16] Theatre conditions on tour can be particularly problematic. I recall, for example, finding my mouth full of knitting when playing Mouth in *Not I* at the Dublin Theatre Festival in 1978. In the very limited set-up time allowed in festival conditions, the hole in the blackout curtain was only cut at the last minute and, there being no suitable material at hand for the mask, the stage manager cut a sleeve from his jersey, made a hole in it and tacked it to the inside of the curtain. In the ensuing performance, on inserting my mouth through the hole, tendrils of wool began to descend, tickling both mouth and nostrils, so that choking, or at least a gigantic sneeze, became genuine possibilities! Again, when playing W in *Rockaby* in Wellington, New Zealand, in 1990, I was almost thrown from the rocking chair when an assistant stage manager suddenly became over-zealous in operating the pulley that controlled the chair. W cannot rock the chair herself, since Beckett specifies that it only moves involuntarily.

Unusual problems largely peculiar to Beckett's theatre may also arise. There is, for example, the difficulty of obtaining the complete darkness often required in the short plays. A total blackout is naturally affected by the glow from the exit lights, which, for legal reasons, must be illuminated throughout a performance. Similarly a long pause in mainstream theatre is quite different from the order of silence that can build up in a Beckett play. When, for example, one of the late plays is working as it should, audiences become rapt, indeed almost hypnotised, so that any extraneous noise, even from outside the theatre, can become audible and intrusive in a way that would not be noticeable on the mainstream stage.

Beckett's short plays present particular challenges to audiences, not least in coming to recognise that the staging and technical effects are being stretched beyond their usual function in the theatre and are an integral part of the performance (such as the use of mid-air as the stage space in *Not I* and the personification of the light in *Play*). There was, of course, an initial lack of comprehension from public and press alike of the 'whatever next?' variety: characters in dustbins, a woman stuck in a mound of earth, heads sprouting from urns, a mouth gabbling in mid-air – 'what's it meant to mean?' (as Beckett himself slyly asks in *Happy Days*). As soon as audiences relax, however, and allow the plays to work on them in their own terms, they find such considerations unimportant and that the plays do communicate with them directly; all the more so for making them concentrate by not dotting all the i's and crossing all the t's. The concentration indeed can become so intense that it is almost palpable, as though the audience were holding its breath.

Naturally with the very short plays a programme must be devised to provide an evening's theatre. At least two plays will be performed, and their grouping can be illuminating. Staging *Footfalls* and *Rockaby* together can work well, both plays being concerned with mother/daughter relationships, or combining *Not I* with *That Time*, which Beckett called 'a brother to *Not I*'.[17] The 30-second *Breath* has even been performed several times in an evening, virtually as punctuation between a group of short plays! The plays work best in smaller theatres, where such minimalist but crucial action as the opening of Listener's eyes in *That Time* can be registered clearly by audiences.

Another method of devising a Beckett evening arose for myself, following an invitation to perform a programme of short plays during a conference of European translators of Beckett's work at the University of East Anglia.[18] In that context it seemed appropriate to experiment by playing *Rockaby* in English, followed by *Berçeuse*, the French version. Having found that the contrasts inherent in seeing a play in two languages interested the audience, I devised a programme which has subsequently toured worldwide, largely to university theatres. This consists of performing the play first in English, followed (after a short break) by the French version. There is then an interval (during which it is advisable to remove the heavy make-up) before returning to the stage to give those among the audience who wish to remain an opportunity to ask questions, or comment on Beckett's theatrical methods. This tends to produce a very lively debate, in that just after the performance of unusual material proves to be an optimum time to engage audiences in discussion, which ranges widely from personal insights to close intellectual enquiry. In Szeged, South Hungary, a student said she had begun to understand her grandmother's gradual withdrawal from the world for the first time; in Strasbourg an Austrian university lecturer felt that the poetic nature of Beckett's language had helped him to come to terms with the recent death of his mother, while several members of the audience in Zurich's Teater Neumarkt, having discussed the linguistic differences between the two languages, were particularly anxious to hear the play again – in German!

The aural contrast between the English version followed by the more liquid-sounding French one also works on another level. Having followed the plot of the English version, the repeat of the play allows even non-French speaking audiences to reflect on it; this has the effect of deepening their experience of the play, much as Beckett intended the *da capo* of *Play* to work on audiences; to let the 'hooks' go in, as he wrote of a production of *Fin de partie*.[19]

On tour the experience of putting on the plays often provided a steep learning curve for the university drama students who assisted. If they were unfamiliar with Beckett's later plays they tended to expect such short texts to present few problems, only to find themselves confronted by the niceties of technical synchronisation, which they found exceptionally demanding; particularly the extent to which their own technical input interacting with the performer constituted the performance. In subsequent discussion it is always rewarding to see their minds opening to the possibilities of minimalist theatre and their developing appreciation of Beckett's dramatic methods.

It may have become apparent that, while discussion so far has centred on the actor, audience and technical aspects of a Beckett performance, there has been little mention of overall direction. This is because I have been positing a director who would follow Beckett's stage directions closely, in order to bring out the nuances of performance and subtlety of suggestion inherent in his stage notes (for example in the passage of time suggested by the faded primary colours worn by the three women in *Come and Go*).

Today, as the legend of Beckett's own productions begins to dissipate through time, directors become less likely to consult his production notebooks[20] and increasingly anxious to 'do their own thing' with Beckett. It is here that a complex dilemma opens up for both current and future performances of the plays and is the subject of continual debate. It is a theatrical commonplace that without change and experiment theatre becomes static and mummified. Once a play is published it ceases in one sense to be the author's property, in that he can no longer exercise full control over it. Shakespeare lives today because he is constantly reinvented. Each generation uses the plays to reflect their own concerns and, though each new emphasis or reshaping will have its critics, new light is often shed on aspects of a Shakespearean text that deepens and enriches audience experience of the plays.

Shakespeare's five acts can accommodate such a translation in terms, but experimenting with Beckett's plays is much more problematic. Beckett did his best in his lifetime to control productions of his plays via his agents. Today the Beckett Estate has an invidious task in deciding whether a performance flouting Beckett's production intentions can go ahead, the notorious removal of Deborah Warner's *Footfalls* from the London stage being a case in point.[21] Two 'camps' exist today: those who think Beckett is best served by close attention to his stage directions and those who feel that experimenting with new ways of performing his plays is the only way to keep them alive. Among the latter is Jonathan Miller, who feels that the Estate's attempts to protect Beckett from experiment will inevitably result in 'dead theatre' – in effect taxing the Estate with murdering the future of Beckett production.[22]

Clearly, attempting to replicate Beckett's own productions exactly is an arid enterprise, leading to stultified theatre. It is impossible in any case, due to different personnel, theatre spaces and the dating effects of time. Nonetheless a production that follows Beckett's stage directions does not have to be a sterile parroting of the past. Provided that the director respects the text and can pass on his enthusiasm to the cast, the chosen play will take life as their own creation, while still keeping close to Beckett's intentions.

In my view, while it may be possible with the longer plays to introduce flexibility into production methods, in the short minimalist plays experimentation generally proves undesirable. Beckett's concern for the human situation is so clearly apparent in the later plays that a director determined to imprint them with his own stamp is likely to arrive at something much *less* than what is already present in the text. In the late plays the text is narrowed down to reflect the bleakest realities of human existence. The protagonist is presented with all choices made, no opportunity for change and nowhere to go but on, as in the last words of the trilogy: 'You must go on, I can't go on, I'll go on.' In *Quad II*, where all colour has drained from the players' costumes and their brisk movement has slowed to a shuffle about the stage, Beckett remarked: 'Good. That's a hundred thousand years later.'[23] The ghostly players are still in progress, still going on.

If a director subverts the minimalist plays (attempting a contemporary relevance, perhaps) it reduces their pre-existing depth and the impact of the plays is lessened. When rehearsing *Footfalls* in 1976, Beckett remarked: 'It's Chamber Theatre and it must be perfect.'[24] As with Beethoven's *Late String Quartets*, the late plays are Beckett's final contribution to the theatre, and who would attempt to change a note of the *Quartets*?

ANTHONY CRONIN

Beckett's trilogy

Herman Melville, the author of *Moby-Dick* and himself a great creative literary artist, said that he would have preferred 'the still, rich utterance of a great soul in repose' to the plays of Shakespeare. In other words, he regretted Shakespeare's creativity, regretted that Shakespeare had invented all those dramatic fictions, with their poisoned sword tips and discovered letters, when he might have expressed his profoundest thoughts and feelings directly and simply, without pretences, masks or personae. But great souls in repose, such as Melville imagined Shakespeare might have been had he not been involved in the turmoil of dramatic creation, are too often inclined to be silent or even tongue-tied souls. Literature has very little tolerance for abstraction, even abstract, distilled wisdom. There is a handful of essayists and aphorists who have tackled experience more directly than the novel or the play seems to do, and whose work can claim to be literature. And some of those who were prepared to face the necessary self-immolations and patient gathering of facts that biography or history involved could claim to have produced works of art. But it is, alas, the case that where the more difficult, murkier, sometimes contradictory and not easily dredged up truths of our being are concerned the prose embodiment in which they are contained usually has to be a fiction. Whatever may be the case with poetry – and I would argue that poetry has much the same problem – for extended prose works one might almost say that artistic truth, unarguable, embodied truth is almost always to be arrived at by the creation of fictions. Only fiction allows for the necessary rearrangements, reorderings and perhaps simplifications and reweightings of human experience which are necessary to get at the kernels of it. Only through the imagined characters of fiction can we reveal without falsification or self-justification the truth about our own experience. And of course, fiction, unlike the other forms I have mentioned, has in abundance the element of play which is one of the great informing elements in all artistic creation, visual, literary and musical.

But the fact that truth is expressed most inclusively through fiction is of course a paradox, and it has irked a number of people, foremost among them Samuel Beckett. In the novels of no other author does hatred for the necessity of creating a fiction shine through so clearly or is detestation of that necessity expressed with so mordant a wit as in the three novels, *Molloy*, *Malone Dies* and *The Unnamable*, usually – though not by him – called the trilogy, which he began in 1947.

The trilogy may be seen as a series of collapses. Almost as soon as a character is invented and a new story embarked on, disgust and boredom set in. Malone, who is evidently, like the others, in some sense a literary artist, creates a character called MacMann and for a while he is happy to tell MacMann's story. But soon MacMann becomes, all too obviously, Malone.

> What tedium. And I call that playing. I wonder if I am not talking yet again about myself. Shall I be incapable, to the end, of lying on any other subject?

In the last book, *The Unnamable*, there are successive collapses of pretence, peelings away, monologue within monologue; and it is here that these successive collapses or subsidences are explained. Molloy crawling in a state of partial paralysis through the forest, on the way to his mother, Malone dying on his bed, the limbless Mahood in his big glass jar under the tarpaulin, Worm, the reduction of them all whom no threat or torment can goad into action or seemingly even bring to life, are all, we now learn, fictional creations of the Unnamable.

But he is not fitted for fictional creation. He cannot keep it up. Pretence or creation is the converse of truth. For that reason, if for no other, it is synonymous with boredom, disgust and collapse. Yet there is an incomprehensible necessity for creation and pretence. All these masks or personae, these attempts to create and sustain fictional identities, surrogates for himself, are, it seems, made at the bidding of an obscure junta of masters whose nature is never clear but whose rule must be obeyed. It is they who have ordered him to create these stories and these storytellers. It is they who compel him to engage in this weary, endlessly renewed frenzy of creativity.

Even this is not all, for behind them there seem to be others, or at least another. And this other, or others, does not/do not want fictions. He or it or they want the truth and are intolerant of lies. And it is this contradiction, this involvement in seemingly contradictory necessities, which is his principal torment, 'A labyrinthine torment that cannot be grasped, or limited, or felt, or suffered, no not even suffered.'[1] There is on the one hand the command to give utterance, to be verbal, even loquacious – in other words, creative. But this loquacity, this creativity, almost necessarily involves fictions – that is, lies. And at the same time there seems to be a command, or a necessity to utter something truthful and important, something which once uttered will give him quittance, will restore him to his primal self:

It is difficult to speak, even any old rubbish, and at the same focus one's attention on another point, where one's true interest lies, as fitfully defined by a feeble murmur seeming to apologize for not being dead. And what it seemed to me I heard then, concerning what I should do, and say, in order to have nothing further to do, nothing further to say, it seemed to me I only barely heard it, because of the noise I was engaged in making elsewhere, in obedience to the unintelligible terms of an incomprehensible damnation. (282)

The Unnamable's obedience to these contradictory commands seems to be a question of expiation. There is some obscure sin, perhaps the sin of mere being, of ever having been, for which amends must be made. And for him at least this expiation 'boils down to a question of words' (308). It could have taken other forms and sometimes he wonders what the form of expiation that is required of him might have been if it had not been a question of words. A simple job, perhaps, sorting and arranging things, or carrying water in a small thimble from one set of containers to another, tanks perhaps secretly connected by underground pipes, so that his work could be undone as rapidly as he did it. But, because of his disabilities, for him it has to be a question of words. The Unnamable after all has no hands, and hence cannot be required to keep up a continuous clapping noise, as if calling the waiter, or legs – and therefore can scarcely be expected to dance the Carmagnole.

This need for expiation of course relates to Beckett's feeling that mere being was itself an offence, a feeling powerfully reinforced by his reading of the German philosopher Arthur Schopenhauer. No doubt his Low Church Irish Protestantism, so near to Calvinism, had something to do with this too. If you were not among the elect, being was an offence. And how could someone of Beckett's temperament feel himself to be among the elect?

Since for Beckett it is a question of words it would seem that this is one of the things the trilogy is about: the position of the artist, more specifically the literary artist, who has been commanded to create works, or seems to have been commanded, by an obscure power or camarilla of powers, but from whom not mere creation alone but also some sort of ultimate truth is demanded. And from the trilogy onwards most of Beckett's works would involve people who are commanded by voices they do not know anything about to give voice themselves, to tell their story – or, perhaps, just any story. And they cannot even be certain that this is the ultimate commandment, for beyond and above the powers that thus command them there would seem to be another or others enjoining them to be silent, or to earn silence by speaking some sort of ultimate truth.

Beckett was a perfectionist. Most artists are; and indeed perfectionism, as in the case of Eliot and Joyce, was a feature of modernism, which rejected both the journeyman's attitude of 'needs must when the devil drives' and the slapdash, hit and miss methods of the great Victorians. But he was a perfectionist to a degree which was unusual and obsessive even among the modernist masters. He yearned for silence, the blank white page, the most perfect thing of all. As an artist he had had more false starts and false beginnings than most. *Molloy* and what followed only became possible 'the day I became aware of my own folly' and began to write 'the things I feel', he was to say in condemnation of all that had gone before.[2] Perhaps this repeated failure made him feel more acutely than most the torment of marred utterance; and also to feel more intensely than others that the object of true achieved utterance is silence – in some sense or other a permission to be silent, whether granted by one's daemon or by some power outside the self. At its simplest a feeling that one has done it. You don't have to try again.

This is something that many artists feel but few have expressed with such intensity and such longing. As if to make that longing clearer, and as if the hope was growing in him that he was about to achieve what he longed for, his works would after a certain point get shorter and shorter, the fact that he was engaged on something whose crown and reward would be silence becoming ever more manifest. In the meantime, utterance, for whatever reason, had to be given. Stories had to be started and kept going. Even Moran, Molloy's counterpart, a man of action, besotted like many of his kind with the thought of his own capacity and asinine in the conviction that capacity and application somehow amount to a morality in themselves, has the same end as the others.

'I have spoken,' he says,

> of a voice telling me things. I was getting to know it better now, to understand what it wanted. It did not use the words that Moran had been taught when he was little and that he in his turn had taught to his little one. So that at first I did not know what it wanted. But in the end I understood this language. I understood it ... all wrong perhaps. That is not what matters. It told me to write the report. Does this mean that I am freer now than I was? I do not know. I shall learn. (*Beckett Trilogy*, 162)

In most cases the commandment seems to be to create as well as to utter: to create characters and circumstances and stories which will put these characters in motion. It is only through such stories that utterance of any length can be achieved, and length certainly seems to be part of what is required. Another demand seems to be for some form of externalisation. The characters must be real fictions, differing from their creator. 'We are getting on,' says Malone after he has created the pimply adolescent called Saposcat. 'Nothing is less like me than this patient, reasonable child, struggling all alone for years to shed a little light upon himself, avid of the last gleam, a stranger to the joys of darkness. Here truly is the air I needed, a lively tenuous air, far from the nourishing murk that is killing me' (178).

Yet the imperatives from which the story-teller suffers and the obscure commandments he seems to have been given are here again contradictory. For somehow the ultimate release is in the discovery of the true self, and the reward of silence is only in the end given to those who have discovered that self and saved it from being lost amid all the confusions of the world. At the very moment of successful creation, Malone reflects: 'If this continues it is myself I shall lose and the thousand ways that lead there. And I shall resemble the wretches famed in fable, crushed beneath the weight of their

Beckett's baptismal certificate, with date of birth recorded, Register, Tullow Church
(courtesy Church of Ireland Representative Church Body Library)

SAMUEL BECKETT

Eleutheria

☆m

LES ÉDITIONS DE MINUIT

Cover of *Eleutheria*, first published in 1995 by Éditions de Minuit, Paris

Peter O'Toole, Eamon Kelly and Donal McCann in *Waiting for Godot*, directed by Sean Cotter, Abbey Theatre, 1969 (courtesy Abbey Theatre)

Left: Programme for Irish translation of *Godot* made by Liam Ó Briain and Sean Ó Carra, directed by Alan Simpson for An Taibhdhearc, 1971 (private collection)

Above: Programme for *Film* and *Play*, directed by Eddie Golden, Peacock, 1967 (courtesy Abbey Theatre)

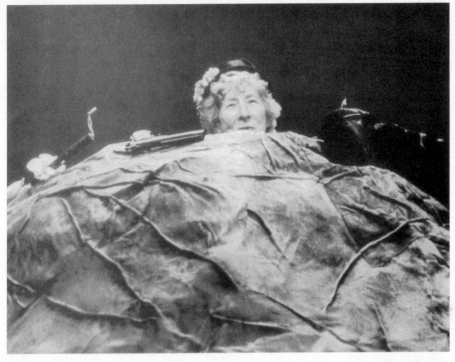

Marie Kean in *Happy Days*, directed by Jim Sheridan, Peacock, 1973 (courtesy Abbey Theatre)

Programme for *That Time*, Peacock, 1978 (courtesy Abbey Theatre)

John Hurt in *Krapp's Last Tape*, directed by Robin Lefèvre, Gate Theatre, 1991 (courtesy Gate Theatre)

Susan Fitzgerald as May in *Footfalls*, directed by Derek Chapman, Gate Theatre, 1991 (courtesy Gate Theatre)

Godfrey Quigley and Barry McGovern in *Endgame*, directed by Ben Barnes, Peacock, 1984
(Photograph: Fergus Bourke)

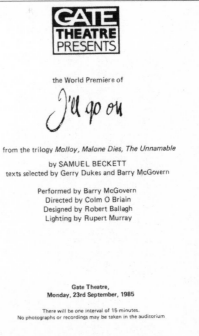

the World Premiere of

I'll go on

from the trilogy *Molloy, Malone Dies, The Unnamable*

by SAMUEL BECKETT
texts selected by Gerry Dukes and Barry McGovern

Performed by Barry McGovern
Directed by Colm O Briain
Designed by Robert Ballagh
Lighting by Rupert Murray

Gate Theatre,
Monday, 23rd September, 1985

There will be one interval of 15 minutes.
No photographs or recordings may be taken in the auditorium

Programme for *I'll Go On*, 1985, one-man show featuring Barry McGovern, adapted from
Beckett's trilogy by Barry McGovern and Gerry Dukes (courtesy Gate Theatre)

Poster/Programme for the San Quentin Drama Workshop production of *Krapp's Last Tape* and *Endgame*, [as] directed by Beckett, 1980 (private collection)

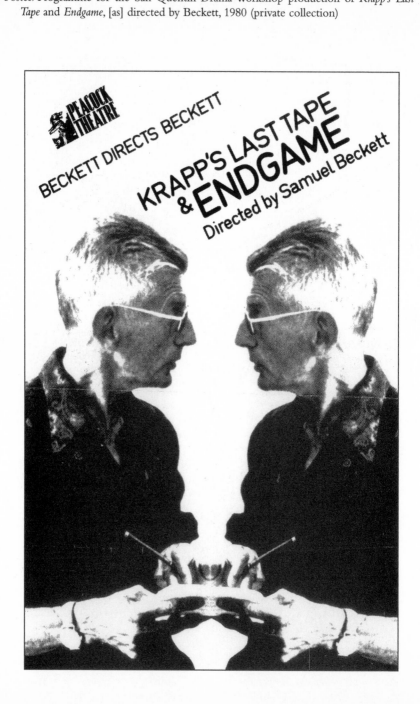

Flo McSweeney as Hands in *Nacht und Träume*,
directed by Sarah-Jane Scaife, Peacock, 1990
(courtesy Abbey Theatre)

Beckett's manuscript entry, 'Da Tagte Es',
from *The Great Book of Ireland/Leabhar Mór
na hÉireann*, 1989 (by permission of the
Trustees). Note that Beckett here transposed
lines 2 and 3 of his poem.

wish come true' (178). But the command to create remains. It is only by the adoption of a fictitious mechanism and the entry into a labyrinth which may never lead back to the self that the self must be revealed. And the fictions thus created must have as much substantive reality as they can be given. The illusion, such as it is, must have some illusory power. Molloy's relationship with his mother, the forest through which he crawls, the fact that Malone is an extremely old man, lying on a bed in a strange room writing the book we are reading with the stub of a pencil (a French pencil, he is careful to assure us), must carry sufficient conviction to enable us to suspend disbelief to the extent that is required. And it is part of Beckett's triumph that his text functions as well as it does on a literal, realistic, or, perhaps one should say, illusionist level while he continually undercuts it as he does.

The principal difficulty here arises from the extreme circumstances in which he places his characters. It is undoubtedly difficult for the reader to believe on any level in these articulate fellows who are yet so reduced in circumstances as to be far beyond the pale of ordinary humanity. Of course we are not required to believe in them in the sense that we would have to if Beckett were a naturalistic novelist with sociological concerns writing stories about *clochards* or tramps and creating what Molloy calls 'a wealth of filthy circumstance'. We are not given any 'filthy circumstance' as to their class background and acquaintance, the events which led them to their present state, et cetera. We are required to take a lot for granted. But we do believe in them on some level or other; that is what story-telling is all about. Some part of Beckett's strength is realism, a savage and exaggerated realism about the body; and an equally uncompromising response to occasional questions about the soul. A great part of his cathartic power lies in these unrelenting reminders. Molloy's relationship with his mother, principally that of a dependant who needs money, Malone waiting for the skinny hand to push in his food and remove his chamber pot, scribbling away meanwhile in his child's exercise book with the stub of that French pencil,

Mahood in his jar on the pavement outside the café – they are all real enough for Beckett's purposes, and while it may not be exactly the realism of Balzac, Flaubert or his friend and mentor James Joyce, whose own work was in many ways the culmination of the realist tradition, it suffices for the sort of conviction as well as for the sort of shock Beckett wishes to produce. Joyce's method was to pile up detail. Beckett's is to strip it away. And by stripping it away, by reducing his characters to the extremer simplicities of need and satisfaction, he succeeds in laying bare some of the realities of the human situation and the grossness of its perhaps necessary illusions.

And there is a bonus in this. Because they are unburdened by social circumstance his characters are free to attain a degree of mere humanness which would otherwise be denied them. The Beckett man belongs to no category, no class, no nationality or community. It is true that, although these novels were first written in French, there is a general background of Irishness, or at least some knowledge of Irish affairs. Moran likes Irish stew and knows something about Irish law. Malone is, like Beckett himself, familiar with the phrase, *Up The Republic!* and aware that it took the Lord Mayor of Cork, Terence MacSwiney, forty days to die on hunger strike. Worm will need his single eye to weep sentimental tears when he 'goes back to Killarney'. MacMann reflects that love will eventually lead him and his Moll hand in hand to a grave in Glasnevin. But these characters are no patriots. Nor do they show much sign of having been brought up by parents or educators in any recognisable system of ethics or morality. Their attitudes are an almost complete reversal of those that most of us have been conditioned to adopt. There is no hitherto esteemed ideal, whether of honour, dignity, trustworthiness, courage, energy, ambition or goodwill, that they have not learned – sometimes by bitter experience – to scorn or disregard. All systems of government are as alien to the Beckett character as he is to them. He believes that most of what we call learning, or science, or philosophy, is a fraud, to be described as time-wasting except that it was probably invented to pass the time. 'Yes,' says Molloy, 'I once took an interest in astronomy, I don't deny it. Then it was geology that killed a few years for me. The next pain in the balls was anthropology' (38).

Born into an unending stream of instruction and exhortation, very likely inaccurate, often maddeningly imprecise, seemingly useless, the Beckett character believes that the most shameful moments in his career were those in which he was deluded enough to try to learn; and he holds by his rejections with a fierce tenacity, often catching himself on in the nick of time, when another than he might have admitted to an emotion or a thought that was, in one way or another, worth the having, or, worse still, to a virtue, such as faith, hope or charity, the most ludicrous of these being hope, a ludicrousness on which, as Beckett well knew, both Schopenhauer, who had been when he read him a revelation, and Proust, the only other author about whom he had ever written at any length, would have been in full agreement.

The Beckett character's experiences of erotic love have certainly not been such as to encourage any belief in it as the great compensatory factor in existence. As MacMann grew more intimate with his Moll, he acquired, we are told, 'some insight into the meaning of the expression, Two is company. He then made unquestionable progress in the use of the spoken word and learnt in a short time to let fall, at the right time, the yesses, noes, mores and enoughs that keep love alive' (239). And he describes his at length successful achievement of some sort of erotic satisfaction as 'a kind of sombre gratification' (238). There is a terrifying passage in which Molloy wonders whether he has ever experienced what the rest of the world calls true love and recounts the experience which he thinks best fits that concept. It was with someone who went by the peaceful name of Ruth, he thinks, but can't say for certain, because perhaps the name was Edith.

Such were the characters that The Unnamable, in obedience to the obscure powers that commanded him, brought into existence in the three books under discussion. Such, through The Unnamable and including that eponymous hero himself, were the characters that Samuel Beckett, a gentle, loving, educated and law-abiding man, brought into existence in obedience to the obscure vocational command that he, like all artists, laboured under.

By 1947, when *Molloy* was begun, the anti-hero had become a familiar figure in European literature, through the abysmally unheroic central character in Dostoevsky's *Notes from Underground*, Flaubert's Bouvard and Pecuchet, Kafka's K and, of course, James Joyce's Leopold Bloom. Of these anti-heroes Beckett's are the ones from whom all vestiges of the heroic or the admirable have been most thoroughly expunged. Thus, while Kafka's K has a highly developed if somewhat neurotic moral sense which makes him anxious to do right and to hope it will be done; and Leopold Bloom, whatever his cowardices and self-abasements, has a great deal of love and fellow feeling in his make-up; the Beckett man is a lone individual who regards all others with fear, hatred, impatience or contempt. And while Kafka's K and Joyce's Leopold Bloom have a certain amount of civic responsibility, the Beckett man has none. He does not believe in the brotherhood of mankind and questions of equality are disposed of by the eager admission that he is, in all respects, inferior. His principal emotion when confronted with humanity at large is fear. 'Morning,' Molloy tells us, 'is the time to hide. They wake up, hale and hearty, their tongues hanging out for order, beauty and justice, baying for their due. Yes, from eight or nine till noon is the dangerous time' (62).

The Beckett man is utterly devoid of ambition and though sometimes, when enraged, he may strike or beat to pulp with his stick or crutches someone even more helpless than himself, he does not seek power over others, or riches or fame. He does not smart under indignity. It is axiomatic with him that one is insulted and humiliated at every turn. He is used to physical suffering and the degradations of the body; indeed he is something of a connoisseur of these and they might almost be said to give him pleasure. When Moran feels the first onset of paralysis in one leg and discovers the joys of immobility, he remarks: 'Such are the advantages of a local and painless paralysis. And it would not surprise me if the great classical paralyses were to offer analogous and still more unspeakable satisfactions. To be literally incapable of motion at last. That must be something! My mind swoons when I think of it' (129).

There remains the question of how far Beckett's people are valid exemplars of humanity, to put it in simple terms, how much of all this is true of the rest of us, true of any of us. In discussing this, or indeed in discussing anything relating to Beckett's vision and purposes, it is essential to emphasise again and again that he is a comic artist and that the basic technique of comedy is exaggeration. Everything in a certain type of comedy, not to say slapstick, is pushed to extremes, extremes of situation, extremes of action, calamity leading to further calamity, the dire situation becoming ever direr. Stephen Leacock, a partially forgotten comic writer about whom Beckett had been enthusiastic as a schoolboy, was a master of this wild progression; and so are almost all the great comic artists of world literature. Another characteristic of the great comic writer is outrage. Comedy, outrageous comedy, is a weapon against lies and concealments, solemnities and pretences; indeed almost the only weapon that can be used without becoming yourself solemn and pretentious, for the comic artist a fate worse than death. For much of its length the trilogy is truly hilarious comic writing. A vein of caustic humour runs through it all, even through the most clogged and complex passages in *The Unnamable*. Its very syntax is a comic device, an exposure of stylistic obsession, of fine writing, of supposed narrative exactitude.

Nevertheless, comic creation or otherwise though the trilogy be, one could argue that the characters in these novels in all their abysmal aspects are at least as true to humanity's real lineaments as most of what has gone before. Most of the great literature of the past deals with the heights of human experience. It took the most exalted moments of lyrical emotion – of love, of sacrifice, even perhaps of hate – and it sought to enshrine them in words which matched their intensity. It celebrated those virtues which were proper to heroic struggle or great achievement – courage and loyalty, will-power, ambition and resolution among them. Even when it dealt in crime or villainy these were not absent. For three thousand years the bias of literature had been tilted one way – towards the heroic and the lyrical-poetic. Now it has been tilted the other, a process which began with the first modern anti-heroes and culminated in Beckett. Deep in our collective soul is a continuous unease about the contrast between the traditional ecstasies, nobilities and romantic passions of literature and what most of us actually feel, the state of mind in which most of us actually live most of the time. And indeed between our portraits of our supposed selves as decent, kind, caring and unselfish and what is actually our psychology, actually our outlook. In its exposure of these gaps, Beckett's trilogy has a profoundly cathartic effect. It may not be all there is to be said, but it is a needed counterbalance to much that has been said. It is a liberation from certain pretences, and, because it is a liberation, the experience of reading *Molloy*, *Malone Dies* and *The Unnamable* is, against all the odds, a joyous and revivifying one.

DERMOT MORAN

Beckett and philosophy

'We always find something, eh Didi, to give us the impression
that we exist.' *Waiting for Godot*
'Mean something! You and I, mean something! [*Brief laugh.*]
Ah, that's a good one.' *Endgame*
'All life long the same questions, the same answers.' *Endgame*[1]

S amuel Barclay Beckett (1906–89) is the most
philosophical of twentieth-century writers. As we hear
from Hamm in *Endgame*: 'I love the old questions. [*With
fervour.*] Ah the old questions, the old answers, there's nothing
like them!' (110). Beckett's writings contain a kind of arbitrary
collection or *bricolage* of philosophical ideas. His characters
exult in endless, pointless, yet entertaining, metaphysical
arguments. His work exudes an atmosphere of existential
angst, hopelessness and human abandonment to the relentless
course of the world. Beckett's characters portray a rootless,
homeless, alienated humanity. One no longer at home in the
world; one lost in a meaningless void. Every play and prose
piece reinforces and deepens this dark diagnosis of the human
condition, generating an overarching world view that has
justifiably been called 'Beckettian' (akin to the 'Pinteresque'

world of Pinter). His 1981 piece *Ill Seen Ill Said* sums up this world as:

> Void. Nothing else. Contemplate that. Not another word.
> Home at last. Gently gently.

Modern humanity is at home in its homelessness. This stark Beckettian world cries out for philosophical interpretation. Indeed in his plays are embedded vague hints and suggestions of deliberate philosophical intent. The outwardly pessimistic atmosphere, the bleak post-apocalyptic landscapes, hopeless characters and the overwhelming sense of the aimlessness and meaninglessness of life, the 'issueless predicament of existence'2 as Beckett himself put it, have led many critics to try to pin down the overall philosophical position to which Beckett supposedly subscribes.

Yet Beckett's relation to philosophy is difficult and complex. He was not a philosopher; if he had been, he would not have needed to engage with art. As an author, he strongly resisted every attempt to impose any philosophical interpretation or meaning on his work. Beckett's answer to philosophy is to refuse it, give it a 'kick in the arse'. His use of ideas is always accompanied by reticence, ambiguity and humorous deflationary counterpoint. Ideas are presented somehow as magnificent edifices that stand apart from the miserable small-mindedness of the human condition. Ideas console, edify, bemuse and entertain, but they are always also misrepresentations, illusions, exaggerations, blinkers, detours that take us blithely beyond the real and pathetic circumstances of our own condition. Thought is a pleasant distraction, but it essentially misleads.

Beckett compounded this refusal to interpret his own work philosophically by claiming not to understand philosophers: 'I never understand anything they write.' And again he wrote: 'I am not a philosopher. One can only speak of what is in front of him, and that is simply a mess.'3

We need then to proceed with caution. To over-emphasise the philosophical in Beckett would be to underplay his deeply serious aesthetic commitment, his lifelong interest in Dante

('Dante's damned'),[4] his admiration for poets such as Rimbaud and Apollinaire, whom he translated, his deep admiration for surrealism, for André Breton and Celine, and, of course, the *nouveau roman* of Alain Robbe-Grillet where objects can be described in a flat neutral tone for pages on end.

Beckett's paradigm of the great artist was James Joyce, whom he regarded as the greatest living prose craftsman and whom he came to know in Paris. These two Irishmen, exiled, living for their art, shared an austere 'art-for-art's-sake' aesthetic that raised the artist up to the quasi-divine craftsman whose work has to stand alone, independent of the world, independent of everyday concern, paring his finger nails, as Joyce put it. Both were devoted to crafting perfect forms, the right words in the right order; or, in Beckett's case, the least number of words and those showing their inadequacy. There is an extraordinarily formal rigour in Beckett as in Joyce. Form is ruthlessly imposed on a wild concoction of different elements. Magpie-like, there is much stealing from music hall, vaudeville, ordinary conversation, philosophical themes, even theology. In his prose especially, Beckett maintains a restrained conversational tone, a detached gentlemanly politeness, even during the most extraordinarily gruelling moments.

Despite their different religious and intellectual formations they were both committed to the religion of art, successors to the Romantic and Symbolist cult of the artist. Although they were both Dubliners, their intellectual backgrounds were quite dissimilar. Joyce had grown up in the Neo-Thomist Catholic intellectual climate at Clongowes, Belvedere and University College, which is deeply informed by the system of Thomas Aquinas, as is evident from the discussion of beauty in *A Portrait of the Artist*. Beckett, on the other hand, was a complete stranger to that world, although he did later try to come to terms with it, reading Dante and Catholic thinkers such as Jacques Maritain.[5] The vision of naked humanity trapped inside a vast cylinder, wandering about searching for a way out, in his 1971 prose piece *The Lost Ones*[6] is reminiscent of the cycles of Dante's *Inferno* and the paintings of Brueghel.

Beckett's bourgeois Protestant outlook, formed in the upper-middle-class suburb of Foxrock, at Portora Royal boarding school in Co. Fermanagh and at Trinity College, was not at all intellectual; it was 'low down Low Church Protestant' as he calls it in *More Pricks Than Kicks*. Indeed, his upbringing and family circumstances reeked of solid, bourgeois respectability, exactly as satirised by Jean-Paul Sartre in his novel *Nausea*. Beckett would fall asleep during sermons in his local church. He was expected to enter the family business of quantity surveying, or settle down as a lecturer at Trinity. But he wanted art, art as a way of transforming if not overcoming personal suffering.

There is undoubtedly a certain psychoanalytic aspect to Beckett's work. His bouts of depression and psychosomatic illnesses led him to London where he was analysed by the famous Freudian analyst Bion. He attended a lecture given by Jung at the Tavistock Centre and later on used the material in one of his works. Jung had talked of someone who gave the impression of never having been fully born, an event that recurs in *All That Fall*.[7]

Beckett's great aesthetic transformation took place when he had the revelation that his art should primarily be drawn from his self-experience. He broke from his artistic torpor and began the extraordinary creative work that would gain him the Nobel Prize for literature in 1969. To look for philosophical commitments outside Beckett's artistic work itself would be to betray its artistic intention and so we should be unsurprised by his silence. Silence and exile, at least, Beckett learned, if not exactly *from*, then at least *alongside*, Joyce in Paris.

Samuel Beckett studied languages, not philosophy, at Trinity College, although his overall academic tutor was A. A. Luce, an authority on the Irish idealist George Berkeley, whose notion *esse est percipi* Beckett's playfully explores in *Film*. Berkeley maintained that matter did not exist; indeed the very notion of matter was, as he put it, 'repugnant', by which he meant 'self-contradictory'. Matter, for the good bishop, was an outrageous invention of scientists and, as such, a great temptation to atheism. Berkeley's response, in defence of theism, is his *immaterialism*, his celebrated doctrine that nothing exists except the mind and its ideas. In short there is God's mind and human minds and God puts the ideas of everything directly into our minds rather than routing it through the medium of an alien matter. To be is to be perceived. Everything that is is an idea in the mind.

Clearly such a position is both deeply eccentric and deeply appealing. Berkeley promoted his outrageous immaterialism with a quite rigorous and impressive battery of arguments, such that he came to represent for many the very paradigm of the solipsistic thinker. Berkeley thought of himself as simply defending common sense. That common sense could in fact be the conduit for such a bizarre idea as that everything in the world is nothing more nor less than the idea we have of it is itself a very challenging thought. Such exuberant ideas offered in the spirit of common sense consolation were Beckett's bread and butter. Berkeley is clearly Beckett's kindred spirit!

Beckett did read philosophy quite intently, especially in the twenties and thirties – notably René Descartes, the father of French philosophy. Descartes was a deeply logical and mathematical thinker who speculated on the possibility that all of experience might be systematically false, misleading as a dream, a delusion brought about by an evil demon who delights in tricking us. Beckett's characters often make reference to Cartesian positions and his characters frequently detach from their pains and emotions in order to comment on them in a dry, analytic manner which makes their calm rationality all the more absurd and disconnected. His characters actually live through the Cartesian divorce of body from mind. The body doesn't do what the mind wants. There is a great deal of solipsistic soliloquy, especially in the novels, so that one can even speak of *Watt* and other novels as explorations of the disembodied, emotionally detached Cartesian subject, albeit always aware of the manner in which soliloquy is also a theatrical artifice.[8]

HAMM: I am warming up for my last soliloquy.[9]

Beckett's first published poem, 'Whoroscope', is based on an early biography of Descartes by Adrien Baillet (1649–1706) in 1691 that Beckett read in Paris. It is a pretentious and somewhat bombastic piece, festooned with learned allusion, adorned with footnotes (following the fashion set by T.S. Eliot), purporting to be in the voice of Descartes himself. It even quotes St Augustine, *si fallor sum*, even if I am in error I am, an earlier version of Descartes' *cogito ergo sum*. Nevertheless, it won a prize of ten pounds in 1930 for the best poem on the subject of time and was published in a limited edition by Nancy Cunard. It is of no philosophical interest, rather it involves Joycean punning combined with veiled allusions to Galileo, Harvey and Franz Hals. The scene in St Augustine's *Confessions* in the garden of his house ('in the shrubbery') where he hears a child singing '*tolle lege*' (take it up and read), and which he takes to be an exhortation to read the Word of Scripture, is rendered in the poem as

He tolle'd and legged
And he buttoned on his redemptorist waistcoat.[10]

Besides Augustine and Descartes, Beckett also read Malebranche and was particularly fascinated by the minor Flemish Cartesian follower and occasionalist Arnold Geulincx (1624–69). Geulincx is the originator of the idea that the relation between the mind and the body is like the relation between two synchronised clocks that exactly agree without influencing each other causally. Geulincx advocated a freedom of the mind that abandons all attempts to influence the course of the mechanistic material world, a condition which aptly describes Molloy, Malone and the other anti-heroes of Beckett's novels.

Not surprisingly, Beckett was also attracted to Arthur Schopenhauer's pessimism. Schopenhauer is referred to in the essay 'Dante ... Bruno. Vico ... Joyce' (1929) that Beckett contributed to the volume *Exagmination*. In his early monograph on Proust Beckett cites Schopenhauer's definition of art as the 'contemplation of the world independently of the principle of reason' and applies it approvingly to Proust.[11] Art tells it like it is, not as it rationally should be.

It was while he was teaching at the Ecole Normale Supérieur in 1928-29 that Beckett read Descartes. Among the elite students there at that time were Jean-Paul Sartre, Maurice Merleau-Ponty and Simone de Beauvoir. Beckett, born in 1906, and Sartre, born in 1905, were almost exact contemporaries. Indeed, Beckett met Sartre at the Ecole Normale and they continued a distant relationship through the forties. Beckett was aware of Sartre's literary reputation and, in 1946, submitted a short prose piece, *Suite* ('Continuation'), and then a series of poems to Sartre's journal *Temps Modernes*.[12] Beckett's experiences with Simone de Beauvoir were somewhat more difficult, as she rejected the second part of *Suite* when Beckett submitted it to *Temps Modernes,* maintaining the first part stood on its own.

Beckett's occasional allusion to philosophers and their ideas is usually casual and playful. For instance, in his first novel, *Murphy*,[13] Neary is a Pythagorean who speaks of *apmonia* (the Greek term for 'harmony, accord'). In *Murphy*, a room is described as windowless 'like a monad', a reference to Leibniz. There is a reference to Zeno as 'that old Greek' in *Endgame*.[14] Beckett's script for his 1964 almost silent *Film*,[15] directed by Alan Schneider and featuring Buster Keaton, opens by directly citing Berkeley: *Esse est percipi*. All extraneous perception suppressed, animal, human, divine, self-perception maintains in being.

Film exploits the relation between perceiver and perceived with a man (Keaton) being pursued by the camera and at certain times (due to the angle of the camera) realising he is 'seen'. There is, as in Sartre's voyeur caught on the stairs looking in the peephole, the unbearability of being perceived, of being objectified. In the case of *Film*, however, perceiver and perceived are the same person; one is in flight from one's own self-perception. But these are fragments, teasers.[16] Later references to philosophy are even more sporadic. Beckett's 1934 poem 'Gnome', already cited in this book, summarises his position towards intellectual learning in those years:

Spend the years of learning squandering
Courage for the years of wandering
Through a world politely turning
From the loutishness of learning[17]

There is no doubt that Beckett did think that much learning was a form of loutishness and continued all his life to savagely dissect and debunk intellectual pretensions.

Merely listing the occasions on which Beckett refers to philosophy, then, would be both tediously pedantic and entirely beside the point. To address the theme of philosophy in Beckett one must do more than rattle off the occasions where philosophy appears in his work.

The theme of Beckett and philosophy can be approached in yet another way. Besides philosophers influencing Beckett, Beckett has also interested – even mesmerised – contemporary philosophers and critics, from Sartre, Lukács and Theodor Adorno to Julia Kristeva,[18] Hélène Cixous, Alain Badiou[19], Gilles Deleuze,[20] George Steiner, Georges Bataille, Maurice Blanchot, Wolfgang Iser, Slavoj Zizek and many others. They have all been attracted to Beckett's relentless vision of the world and our human place in it. They have sought to reflect on Beckett's meaning from quite divergent points of view,[21] seeking to recruit Beckett to one cause or other: from modernism to postmodernism, from structuralism to deconstruction.

Sartre, himself the author of existential plays such as *Huis Clos* (1944), saw himself as engaged with his fellow dramatist Beckett in a common cause of producing a drama that 'decentralised the subject'.[22] The Hungarian Marxist critic Georg Lukács saw Beckett's work as exemplifying capitalist decadence and abstract bourgeois individualism. The German

Jewish philosopher and critical theorist Theodor Adorno, however, strongly disagreed with Lukács. *Endgame* in particular had a very powerful impact on Adorno, who saw in Beckett a kind of 'organised meaninglessness'.[23] For him, Beckett exposes the bankruptcy of philosophy 'as the dreamlike dross of the experiential world and the poetic process shows itself as worn out'.[24] Beckett identifies the tedium of spirit of our late age. For Adorno, Beckett portrays the 'irrationality of bourgeois society on the wane' and the manner it resists being understood.[25] According to Adorno, Beckett's work also challenges and overcomes the individualist ethics underlying existentialism.

Of course, Adorno too overreaches. When Beckett met Adorno in Germany, the philosopher frustrated the dramatist by insisting that Hamm in *Endgame* was short for 'Hamlet' and that 'Clov' was a 'clown' and so on. Despite being corrected by Beckett, who repudiated any such deliberate allusion, Adorno persisted to give this explanation in his speech. Beckett commented sarcastically on the ability of science to progress by self-correction.

The French deconstructionist Jacques Derrida felt so close to Beckett that he was unable to write about him at all,[26] and Richard Kearney, in an insightful essay in *The Irish Mind*, sees Beckett as close to Derrida in pursuing a kind of deconstruction.[27] For his part, Gilles Deleuze speaks of an 'aesthetic of exhaustion' in his long essay on Beckett.

The French poet and critic Maurice Blanchot, writing on *The Unnamable*, sees Beckett as exploring the point of origin of the creative process, the experience of origin which risks negating the self.[28] Blanchot raises the question of who is speaking in Beckett's works. For Blanchot, it is not Beckett, but the urge to speak of language itself. In an earlier 1943 essay, 'From Dread to Language', in *Faux Pas,* Blanchot himself speaks of the writer who finds himself in this more and more comical position of having nothing to write, of having no means of writing it and of being forced by an extreme necessity to keep writing it. This effectively states Beckett's position. There is no doubt too that Beckett himself tried to frame an aesthetic, somewhat in advance of his main work. There is his famous German Letter written to Axel Kaun[29] in 1937 where he tries to suggest that the true power of art is to show up the failure of language. He is seeking to break through language to whatever (being or nonbeing) lies beneath. It is to be a literature of the 'unword'. Blanchot suggests that the 'I' who speaks in Beckett's novels is attempting to reassert mastery over a world and over its own experience when such is plainly impossible. According to Wolfgang Iser,[30] too, in Beckett's trilogy of novels, the first-person narrator gradually retreats into anonymity. The attempt at self-observation leads inevitably into fiction: 'Saying is inventing' as Molloy says.[31]

The theatre critic Martin Esslin has perhaps been most successful in grouping Beckett with Ionesco and Genet as part of the 'theatre of the absurd', using the concept of the absurd as defined by Ionesco:

> Absurd is that which is devoid of purpose [...] Cut off from his religious, metaphysical and transcendental roots, man is lost; all his actions have become senseless, absurd, useless.[32]

These diverse approaches certainly highlight aspects of Beckett's work. But I tend to agree with Beckett that we should resist any one-sided monolithic interpretation of his complex work. Certainly there is no shortage of big ideas in Beckett. His work in one way or another undoubtedly engages in the great themes of philosophy – the meaning of life in the absence of God, suffering, the nature of hope and disappointment, human nature, the condition of embodiment, the experience of being born, dying and just living, the search for value, the human capacity for thought and action or inaction, the nature of time, the poverty of language, the failure of art and so on. It is also undoubtedly true that contemporary philosophy, e.g. Nietzsche's nihilism, Sartre's and Camus' existentialism, Wittgenstein's relentless formalism and modernism, Heidegger's conception of man as existence (*Dasein*) and as being-towards-death, Blanchot's and Derrida's dissections of the failure of language, can shed light on aspects of Beckett.

But there is the danger here, which Beckett rightly sensed, of bypassing the works themselves in favour of some 'big idea' – translating Beckett into philosophy. Overemphasising the supposed philosophical message of Beckett's plays tends to downplay their extraordinary humour and anarchic subversion of any overarching fixed meaning. *Waiting for Godot* is billed by the author as a 'tragi-comedy' and all through Beckett's novels his mordant wit is combined with a playful delight in absurd comic routines that Beckett borrowed heavily from vaudeville theatre and the silent movies – Chaplin, Buster Keaton, later the Marx brothers, in his sequences of hat exchange in *Godot*, distributing sucking-stones between pockets in a fixed manner in *Molloy*, eating bananas in *Krapp's Last Tape*. Nothing is funnier than unhappiness, as we learn in *Endgame*. This relentless black humour supplies the transcendence lacking in the attempted philosophical justifications.

Of course, this humour is tempered by his recurrent sepulchral and at times even almost apocalyptic imagery of unyielding grey light, ashes, sand, fallen leaves ... Life is like that, veering haphazardly from the tragic to the ridiculous. In reaction to this, Beckett lets the voices of the mundane penetrate the rarefied atmosphere of the conceptual systems. He won't yield to the seduction of the big, comforting philosophical speculation. The world is a world of the small, the displaced, the *clochard*, us. In *Waiting for Godot* Pozzo inspects the two tramps Vladimir and Estragon and says they are human beings, of the same species as myself, 'made in God's image', a remark whose theological resonance is undercut by the scene of dishevelled humanity before our eyes.

In illustration of the manner in which the philosophical sublime is traduced by the mundane, let us examine Beckett's treatment of three different themes – time, reason and language.

A major *topos* in Beckett is the experience of time, a topic that intrigued philosophers from Plato and Augustine to Henri Bergson, William James and Martin Heidegger, not to mention writers such as Proust, Joyce and Virginia Woolf.[33] Beckett's time is quotidian, empty, repetitive and vacuous. It does not lead to the Pauline and Heideggerian moment of insight and decision. It just goes on.

> HAMM: What time is it?
> CLOV: The same as usual.[34]

Portentous remarks like: 'we are born astride of a grave', are undercut by comic observations:

> VLADIMIR: That passed the time.
> ESTRAGON: It would have passed anyway.[35]

Clearly, *Waiting for Godot* may be seen as explorations of the condition of *waiting* (Heidegger writes analogously on the phenomenon of boredom). By the condition of waiting, I mean that there is a phenomenon of experiencing time in a certain mode, the mode of expectation. As the philosopher critic Günther Anders puts it, in *Godot* there is a sense that 'we remain, therefore we must be waiting for something'.[36] But waiting does not have a theological gloss. The prisoners of San Quentin prison were treated to a performance of *Waiting for Godot* in 1957 and they grasped what the sophisticated New York audiences had not, namely that the play is about what it is like to wait: waiting for release; an expectation they know will be disappointed.[37]

Ironically, we know from John Calder, Beckett's publisher and friend, that Beckett himself was extremely punctilious in all his business appointments and could not stand someone being late.[38] We are always waiting for something to happen. We are waiting for school to be over, for work to finish, for love to arrive, for Christmas to arrive, summer to come, war to begin, war to end, death to come, dying to be over. It is this constant waiting in human life that is given theological interpretation as waiting for salvation, waiting for the Redeemer to come. Beckett's response is to go for the cheap laugh, pull the music hall stunt:

CLOV: Do you believe in the life to come?
HAMM: Mine was always that.[39]

Time is always the same time, the usual. But there is another kind of experience dominant in Beckett and that is the nature of hope and disappointment and the operation of chance in our lives. One of the thieves was saved; one was damned. 'It's a reasonable percentage,' Estragon comments in *Waiting for Godot*.[40] But doubts are raised; because only one of the four Evangelists mentions the thief who is saved. Why believe one out of four? An unreasonable percentage.

Beckett's characters always enjoy absurd speculation pursued and defended with a rigorous logic. In *Waiting for Godot* Vladimir and Estragon engage in speculation and then they argue:

ESTRAGON: That's the idea, let's contradict each other.[41]

There is a wonderful passage in the novel *Malone Dies*[42] where Malone, confined to his bed, is reduced to finding things and exploring his space with his walking stick. His only other possession is a pencil. He records his day to day decline with a kind of clinical detachment. Then one day he loses his walking stick. This gives him an opportunity to engage in a marvellous metaphysical reflection on the manner in which reason transcends the mundane to contemplate, in detached Platonic manner, the *essence*:

I have lost my stick. That is the outstanding event of the day, for it is day again. The bed has not stirred. I must have missed my point of purchase, in the dark. *Sine qua non*, Archimedes was right. The stick, having slipped, would have plucked me from the bed if I had not let it go. It would of course have been better for me to relinquish my bed rather than to lose my stick. But I had not time to think. The fear of falling is the source of many a folly. It is a disaster. I suppose the wisest thing now is to live it over again, meditate upon it and be edified. It is thus that man distinguishes himself from the ape and rises, from discovery to discovery, ever higher, towards the light. Now that I have lost my stick I realize what it is I have lost and all it meant to me. And thence ascend, painfully, to an understanding of the Stick, shorn of all its accidents, such as I had never dreamt of. What a broadening of the mind. So that I half discern, in the veritable catastrophe that has befallen me, a blessing in disguise. How comforting that is. Catastrophe too in the ancient sense no doubt. To be buried in lava and not turn a hair, it is then a man shows what he is made of. To know you can do better next time, unrecognizably better, and that there is no next time, and that it is a blessing there is not, there is a thought to be going on with. I thought I was turning my stick to the best possible account, like a monkey scratching its fleas with the key that opens its cage. For it is obvious to me now that by making a more intelligent use of my stick I might have extracted myself from my bed and perhaps even got myself back into it, when tired of rolling and dragging myself about the floor or on the stairs. That would have introduced a little variety into my decomposition.[43]

The image of reason being used by humans for a perfectly satisfying but wholly inadequate purpose, scratching oneself, is magnificent. In *Waiting for Godot* Estragon has no doubt why people choose to believe the one Evangelist who writes of the thief that was saved as opposed to the three who did not mention this: 'People are bloody ignorant apes'.[44]

Beckett exults in the manner in which this meandering reflection can both satisfy and annoy. Thought is, to adapt Marx's phrase, 'the opium of the people'. Recall Beckett's translation of Sébastien Chamfort's short prose pieces, 'Huit Maximes' ('Eight Maxims'):

> La pensée console de tout et remédie à tout. Si quelquefois
> Elle vous fait du mal, demandez-lui le remède du mal q'elle
> Vous a fait, elle vous le donnera.

Literally translated this poem reads:

> Thought consoles all and heals all. If sometimes
> It does you wrong, ask it to heal the wrong that it has done you,
> It will give that to you.

Beckett's translation, of course, compresses this much further into a rather more austere if traditional rhyming couplet:

Ask of all-healing, all-consoling thought
Salve and solace for the woe it wrought.

Thought damages us, but it also distracts. Beckett's characters regularly try to think or remember having thought or wonder whether thought is possible.

There is a moment in the second act of *Waiting for Godot* where Vladimir and Estragon are waiting by the tree and they make an effort to 'converse calmly since we are incapable of keeping silent':

ESTRAGON: It's so we won't think.
VLADIMIR: We have that excuse.
ESTRAGON: It's so we won't hear.
VLADIMIR: We have our reasons.
ESTRAGON: All the dead voices.
VLADIMIR: They make a noise like wings.
ESTRAGON: Like leaves.
VLADIMIR: Like sand.
ESTRAGON: Like leaves.
Silence[45]

They enter into a discussion to stop thinking. They agree to contradict each other and that diversion continues for a while with Estragon proclaiming: 'That wasn't such a bad little canter'.[46] Thinking is 'not the worst'.[47] The servant/slave Lucky, according to his master Pozzo, 'used to think very prettily once'.[48] He is invited to think as a form of entertainment (to pass the time). Lucky cannot think without his hat on. But then he bursts forth in a terrifying monologue that Beckett's stage directions describe as a 'tirade'. Lucky's 'think' is an incoherent rant framed in a scholarly and quasi-legalistic language, invoking the attributes of God 'outside time without extension' – his lack of time, speech, action, feeling, *apathia*, *aphasia*, *athambia*, metaphysical notions like *esse in posse* (being in possibility) and the 'good Bishop Berkeley' but it is also peppered with autobiographical allusion (including the name Cunard and listing games from golf to tennis):

> Given the existence as uttered forth in the public works of Puncher and Wattmann of a personal God quaquaquaqua with white beard quaquaquaqua outside time without extension who from the heights of divine apathia divine athambia divine aphasia loves us dearly with some exceptions for reasons unknown but time will tell are plunged in torment plunged in fire whose fire flames if that continues and we can doubt it will fire the firmament that is to say blast hell to heaven so blue still and calm so calm a calm which even though intermittent is better than nothing but not so fast and considering what is more that as a result of the labours left unfinished crowned by the Acacacacademy of Anthropopopometry of Essy-in-Possy of Testew and Cunard it is established beyond all doubt all other doubt than that which clings to the labours of men that as a result of the labours unfinished of Testew and Cunard it is established as hereinafter but not so fast for reasons unknown that in view of the labours of Fartov and Belcher left unfinished for reasons unknown ...[49]

As Beckett knew, philosophers, theologians and lawyers love that little Latin word '*qua*', or 'as'. One can think of Jesus as man or as God, *qua* man, *qua* God. But this clever splitting of meaning does not result in a refined system, rather it produced a mess.

Beckett's aesthetics, as he explained in his conversation with Georges Duthuit, is based on the artist renouncing his/her traditional mastery over creation. Instead, art should now draw attention to its own failure to express and to the fact there is nothing to express. Beckett's poetic and dramatic exploration of the essential failure of art and of language brings him closest to contemporary philosophy, whether to Wittgenstein's *Tractatus*' proclamation 'whereof one cannot speak, thereof one must be silent', or Heidegger's reflections on the failures of inauthentic idle talk in *Being and Time*, or in the post-modern meditations on language's lack of origin and failure to refer. How do words refer? How does language hook onto the world? Beckett's art at the same time isolates and inhibits the move to complete expression of meaning. He recognises the inescapable need to say, to name, to put the word on it. He puns on the very phrase 'needless to say'.

Beckett's last stuttering poem '*Comment dire*' (what's the word) written in October 1988 encapsulates this search for the right word, trying to say, seeming to glimpse the word.

> glimpse—
> seem to glimpse—
> need to seem to glimpse—
> afaint afar awayover there what—
> folly for to need to seem to glimpse afaint afar awayover there
> what—
> what—
> what is the word—
>
> what is the word—[50]

Beckett becomes less tolerant with words and their limitations, their poverty, not — as in Joyce — their rich polysemy. Yet he also exults in words, in the poetry of disrupted expression. His late prose pieces reverse grammatical order, breaking the stranglehold of grammar over linguistic expression.

It is wrong to think of Beckett as having a simple philosophical message and especially a bleak one. Rather Beckett's experience is of a world lacking any overall, final meaning. It is not even, as Hobbes asserted, that life is nasty, brutish and short. Rather, it simply goes on. Beckett remains fascinated with the way life continues:

> What counts is to be in the world, the posture is immaterial, so long as one is on earth. To breathe is all that is required, there is no obligation to ramble, or receive company ...[51]

Life ticks on through the boredom of youth and the loneliness of old age. But in all that tedium, there is, especially in the novels and plays, in Beckett an almost manic, exulting joy. Life is like that. Take it or leave it. But enjoy the joke.

R ICHARD
K EARNEY

imagination wanted:
dead or alive

My first impressions of Beckett were very unimpressive. In fact I found him a pompous bore. I first encountered him in his poetry in the 1970s. I'd bought his slim *Collected Poems,* containing a long poem written in one day on 15 June 1930 when Beckett was still a student in Trinity College. It sported the clever and somewhat cheeky title 'Whoroscope', a mixed pun on whore and horoscope. I myself was a young student at UCD and bought the book as a birthday present for my friend Ronan Sheehan. On my way to his Dublin home to deliver the gift, I started reading the volume on the bus and immediately found myself recoiling from Beckett's stiff, arcane verse penned in a pretentiously Italianate style. I presented the gift to my friend anyway; but I felt a little guilty, not only for having read it beforehand but for still offering it as a present after having found it so unpalatable.

My second encounter with Beckett was hardly much better. This time it was his early prose essays on Joyce and Proust. Again I found the material indigestible in the extreme – morbid pseudo-intellectualism allergic to the joys of existence and desperate to impress. The person Beckett was especially trying to win over was, of course, his then mentor and role model, James Joyce, whose unofficial Paris secretary – the term is not quite right – he had just become. But to Beckett's chagrin it was less Joyce's attentions he managed to secure than those of his highly strung daughter, Lucia, who became quite smitten with the newly arrived Dubliner.

My third encounter with Beckett was more personal but no less dispiriting. When travelling to Paris one summer I was encouraged by the poet John Montague to visit Beckett in his Rue St Jacques apartment with a view to conducting an interview for the Irish journal *The Crane Bag*, which I was co-editing at the time. I duly wrote to Beckett requesting the favour of a brief meeting. Within days I received a curt and cryptic reply. It culminated with the unambiguous line: '*merci mais non merci*'. Thanks but no thanks. That's just about how I felt about Beckett too at the time.

Fortunately, that was not the end of the story. Were it so, I would not be delivering this Thomas Davis lecture today. Everything changed for me one year in the mid-seventies when I had the good fortune to see a number of wonderful productions of Beckett plays in Dublin. The first I remember was *Endgame* by UCD Dramsoc. This was followed by *Happy Days* and *Waiting for Godot*. There were some hugely gifted actors and directors at college at that time – including Dermot Moran, Jim Sheridan, Joe Long, Gerry McNamara and Cathy Leeney – but I cannot recall who exactly played what roles in those plays. All I remember, and remember vividly to this very day, was the *humour*. The laughing out loud from the pit of my being. The irony, the satire, the parody, the hilarity – and, above all, the irrepressible sense of humanity in the face of pain and paralysis. Sitting there in the dark theatre my ear suddenly became attuned to another frequency, a strangely new acoustic. I was at last beginning to get it, to hear the tones, inflections and nuances of the distinctively Beckettian voice. The word had finally become flesh for me, incarnate in the ingenious repartee of those moving, struggling, suffering but unsurrendering characters. I can still see their ragged shapes shuffling about in the tacky amateur conditions of a Belfield Basement, the notorious LG1. A new world opened up for me: the world of Beckett's imagination.

After the magic of the plays came the comic brio of the novels. I recall feelings of irrepressible mirth as I read of Murphy turning right down a Dublin street as his mind decided to turn left, thereby illustrating the absurdity of Descartes' claim that the mind (as thinking *cogito*) is dualistically separated from the body (as extended matter). Or the character deputed but miserably failing to flush the ashes of a recently deceased friend down the toilet bowl of the old Abbey Theatre. Or Molloy as he engaged in the crazy antics of sucking stones in logical sequence, or relieving himself on the sports pages of *The Irish Times*. All these vice-narrators, as Beckett liked to call his loquacious soliloquists, were up to no good but they rarely committed evil. They were, to a man, woman and child, human – *all too human. Des hommes moyens sensuels.* Guys in the street. The descendants of Molly and Bloom with a dash of Irish Protestant melancholy and a large dose of enlightenment rationalism (brought to parodic extremes). As Beckett himself once put it, 'when you are in the last ditch, only one thing is left – to sing'.[1] Beckett's characters did just that. They couldn't go on – for there was no good reason for going on – but they went on just the same. And as they hobbled along their forsaken boreens, they conjured up words of dark beauty in the midst of loss. They made, like the dead voices in *Godot*, noises that sounded now like leaves, now like sand, now like leaves again … Haunting stuff.

But for me – as a philosopher – the work of Beckett's that intrigued me most in the end was a short text entitled *Imagination Dead Imagine*. This little prose experiment is less a novel than a post-novel. Or better still, a postscript to a novel. First published in 1965 it was one of a number of minimalist exercises that Beckett called variously 'texts for nothing', 'residua' or simply '*textes manqués*' (failed texts). It corresponded very much to Beckett's deep literary conviction, expressed in various exchanges with friends and interviewers, that if Joyce represented a literature of *omnipotence*, his own work should be read – contrariwise – as a literature of *failure*. Or as Beckett put it in his conversation with one critic, his work was concerned with exploring the contemporary 'rupture of the lines of communication'. There was, he explained, nothing left to express and no way to express it. All that remained was to bear witness to the simultaneous 'breakdown of the object' and collapse of the author's interior existence.[2]

This had radical implications for what was generally meant by the term imagination. Beckett was certainly determined to deconstruct the popular romantic view that imagining is a way in which the writer's will imposes itself on the world and on others, reducing the enigmas and contingencies of reality to one's own fantasies and projections. This attitude of 'voluntary imagination' he denounced as the tyranny of the 'eye of prey'. Against this, Beckett championed the operations of involuntary experience celebrated by Proust. Only by overcoming our willful imagination, it seemed, could we remain fully attentive to the 'suffering of being'[3] which, for Beckett, constitutes the irreducible truth of existence. Hence the move to declare imagination dead!

But Beckett realised that even such a strategy was doomed to failure. For in imagining imagination dead are we not still imagining? There is no way to escape imagination. So the question then arises: can we somehow redeploy imagining so that it respects the 'suffering of being' and avoids the imperiousness of romantic egotism? That was the key challenge for the author of *Imagination Dead Imagine*.

Before proceeding to this text, however, let me pause for a moment to unpack Beckett's pivotal distinction, in his early essay on Proust in 1931, between voluntary and involuntary images. Whereas the involuntary yields to a genuine 'revelation of reality', the voluntary, he writes, 'is of no value as an instrument of evocation and provides an image [...] far removed from the real'.[4] The danger of much modern and romantic literature, according to the young Beckett, is that it ignored the true otherness of being by transforming experience into an aesthetic projection of the author. In one particularly trenchant passage, Beckett seems to be prefiguring the postmodern call for a debunking of the humanist imagination when he declares that 'art', which had for centuries been revered as the 'one ideal and inviolate element in a corruptible world', is in fact quite as 'unreal and sterile as the construction of a demented imagination'.[5] No amount of creative human activity could, it seems, recreate a genuine experience of things. The fictional imagination thus appears to be little more than a distortion, a process wherein a human self forges the world according to its own preconceived image. The voluntary imagination is denounced accordingly by the angry young Beckett as the 'inevitable gangrene of romanticism'. The mere 'dream of a madman'. He concludes: 'imagination, applied *a priori* to what is absent, is exercised *in vacuo* and cannot tolerate the limits of the real'.[6]

This position results in a deep paradox at the heart of Beckett's own writing, namely, the attempt to dismantle fiction by means of fiction. 'The same lie lyingly denied,' as he expressed it in the thirteenth of his *Texts for Nothing*.[7] Hence we find so many of Beckett's narrators − or vice-narrators as he liked to call them − undermining their own narratives from Krapp and Estragon to Murphy and Malone. They generally did this by means of cynical and self-negating asides such as 'This is awful writing' or 'What a misfortune, the pen must have slipped from my fingers' and so on. Indeed, this performative contradiction is brought to the point where traditional notions of authorship, narration, character and plot began to collapse altogether. One even finds narrators of one text referring across to narrators in other texts, creating the impression that literature is like one big labyrinth of mirrors, a panelled cave of echoes, a padded cell of repetitions from which there is no exit. Take this typical passage, for example: 'But let us leave these morbid matters and get on with that of my demise, in two or three days, if I remember rightly. Then it will all be over with the Murphys, Merciers, Molloys, Morans and Malones, unless it goes on beyond the grave.'⁸ Even the self-parodying imagination cannot, it seems, escape itself. The crime of fiction – which Beckett seems to equate here with lying, illusion and evasion – returns to plague the inventor, just like Prometheus, a favourite hero of Beckett's narrators, who stole the fire of imagination from the gods only to be plagued by a vulture sent down by Zeus to torture him every day. Once one enters the fictional hall of mirrors there seems to be no way out.

In this sense, we could read Beckett's writings as a series of ironic attempts to bring imagination to an end. Exercises in terminal fiction without termination, so to speak. Why? Because fiction is, for Beckett, a self-reflexive play which cannot undo itself except by inventing another fiction – and so on *ad infinitum*. It is as self-defeating as trying to quench your thirst by drinking sea-water. The more you satiate your craving the more the craving grows. It is in this context that we might best understand Beckett's advocacy of an aesthetic of failure in his famous 1949 dialogues with George Duthuit for the Paris journal *transition*. He seems here to be making a virtue of necessity, testifying to the impotence of the artist to transcend art by paradoxically exposing its own artifice. Here is one particularly revealing passage:

> to be an artist is to fail, as no other dare fail, that failure is his world and the shrink from it desertion. [...] I know that all that is required now, in order to bring this horrible matter to an acceptable conclusion, is to make of this submission, this admission, this fidelity to failure, a new occasion, a new term of relation, and of the act which unable to act, obliged to act, he makes, an expressive act, even if only of itself, of its impossibility, of its obligation.⁹

The impossibility of imagination to escape from itself is the main theme of *Imagination Dead Imagine*. The self-regarding irony of the title makes this clear. The text takes the form of a monologue in which an unnamed narrator describes a rotunda-shaped skull (the narrator's own head seen from the inside?). The outer world is reduced to a pulsing white light that comes and goes. We find ourselves in a colourless, expressionless space – Beckett's chosen metaphor for the postmodern imagination condemned to itself. All that seems to remain of western humanist culture is this anonymous place where the time-honoured distinction between the imaginary and the real has collapsed. Imagination has, it seems, self-destructed into a void. It has ceased to operate as a human agency of expression, will and creativity and become instead a mechanical pulse of repetition. Even the two white auto-matons slowly expiring within the rotunda are mere doubles of each other, lying back to back, head to tail, in a condition of suspended animation; the only hint of life is to be found in mist on mirrors held before their faces. (It is hard not to think of the final scene in *King Lear*.) These mute doubles of the dying imagination are disconcertingly inhuman. They might well pass for inanimate, the text tells us, 'but for the left eyes which at incalculable intervals suddenly open wide and gaze in unblinking exposure long beyond what is humanly possible. [...] The faces too, assuming the two sides of a piece, seem to want nothing essential.'[10] Struck by the terrible silence and immobility of these moribund marionettes, the narrator can still remember a time when things were otherwise. But it is no more than a memory, a vague recall, a remembrance evacuated of images. And there is, apparently, no way back to that past. And no way forward either. The narrator is caught in the paralysis of an immutable present that is eternally recurring. Hell on earth.

We, the readers, are thus confronted with a strange phantas-magoria which refuses to translate itself into recognisable human forms. We are exposed to a scene which frustrates our natural desire for representation, meaning, expression. Even action – the basic ingredient of any story as Aristotle recognised in the *Poetics* – seems impossible. Plot has become a parody of itself, pitilessly reduced to the technical repetition of an algebraic formula. But this entropic decline of imagination into emptiness cannot even rely on the finality of death as a solution. What we have is an ending without end, an apocalypse without apocalypse. For even as we imagine imagination dead, we still find ourselves caught in the reflexive spiral of imagining. Life and death have become indifferent, indistinguishable. 'No trace anywhere of life,' the narrator tells us at the outset (182), 'you say, pah, no difficulty there, imagination not dead yet, yes, dead, good, imagination dead imagine.' Indeed, he finds the world 'still proof against ending tumult. Rediscovered miraculously after what absence in perfect voids it is no longer quite the same, from this point of view, but there is no other' (184).

That last phrase says it all. There is no *other*: no other perspective, no other reality, no other world, no other being *tout court* – animal, human or divine. Only a dying imagination which cannot die, one moment affirming that 'there is better elsewhere', only to deny it the next, 'there is nothing elsewhere'. The age-old metaphysical quest for some original experience, some lost holy grail, some transcendental truth, seems irreversibly suspended, 'and no question now of ever finding again that white speck lost in whiteness'(185).

Reading these lines I was reminded of Herman Melville's terrifying description of the all-consuming, neutralising whiteness of the whale in *Moby-Dick* – what he termed that 'colorless all-color of atheism'. Or the famous passage in the *Gay Science* where Nietzsche declares how the 'death of God' exposes us to a blank universe where, as he puts it, 'we have unchained this earth from its sun [...] moving continually backward, forward, in all directions [...] straying as through an infinite nothing [...] feeling the breath of empty space?'[11]

The way that Beckett plays with the solar image is significant I think. The use of the sun as metaphor for the ultimate origin of light and warmth was a key figure in Plato and the entire history of western philosophy. For Plato and the ancient Greeks the sun symbolised that otherworldly source of truth which the human imagination sought to faithfully copy. As M.H. Abrams's *The Mirror and the Lamp* (1953) has accustomed us to think, with the modern turn towards romanticism and existentialism the metaphor of the sun still dominated though with this crucial difference: it was now celebrated as a *lamp* within the human imagination which projected light and meaning onto the world, rather than as a passive *mirror* that simply imitated a transcendental form that pre-existed it. This turn from the mimetic imagination of antiquity to the productive imagination of modernity was what Emmanuel Kant called the 'Copernican revolution' in western thought.

In Beckett, it seems, we have a radical reversal of both versions of the solar image – premodern and modern. For in Beckett's postmodern scenario it is no longer possible to trace the 'rise and fall' of the sun back to any origin whatsoever. Neither back to a divine transcendental source *above* us (as in Plato), nor to a human transcendental source *within* us (as in Kant and the romantics). Instead we find a sunless light which comes and goes from *nowhere*. We cannot tell whether it comes from within the white skull of imagination or from without. 'The light that makes all so white no visible source, all shines with the same white shine, ground, wall, vault, bodies, no shadow' (*Imagination Dead Imagine* 182). Indeed the ostensible movement of this pseudo-sun itself – 'from white and heat to black and cold, and vice versa' (183) – defies all human expectations. As soon as you think you have tracked its course, it reverses and undoes its own trajectory: 'the rise now fall, the fall rise'. Imagination is thus reduced to a skeleton of itself – imagining, as it were, its own posthumous existence, its life after death. In other words, no longer able to represent the transcendental sun in mimetic copies (as in Platonism) or to project the sun's light from within its own creative subjectivity (as in romanticism), the postmodern imagination of Beckett's text becomes the pawn of an electronically computerised system – a world where an artificial light comes and goes according to a logic of mathematical precision and technical reversibility which it is beyond the powers of a human self to control or comprehend.

So, is Beckett then an inveterate pessimist? A dour old nihilist? A disconsolate Dubliner without love or hope? Is that the sorry conclusion we must draw from this curious text? The matter is not so simple. In fact, if Beckett is saying, in one breath, that imagination is dead even as it lives, with the other he is countering: imagination lives even as it appears to die! Like the two partners in the rotunda skull, there are two sides to Beckett's story: one tragic, the other comic; one despondent, the other defiant. The imaginary scenario depicted here, like most of Beckett's other texts, is suspended half-way between a grave and a womb (to borrow one of his most famous images from *Godot*). One moment, the figures in the white zone resemble half-dead corpses, the next living embryos. This paradoxical attitude is succinctly summed up, I think, in Beckett's heart-felt confession of never knowing for certain but always hoping against hope: 'Where we have both dark and light, we have also the inexplicable. The key word in my plays is "perhaps".'[12] And not just in the plays, I would suggest.

Beckett's work has, I believe, a particular resonance for our time. And a very special relevance too. His depiction of an undecidable zone between the imaginary and the real is arguably a prophetic prefiguration of the virtual world of anonymous high-tech communications in which we now find ourselves. A world where so much of our experience is disembodied, vicarious and impersonal (how many people's lives today are lived in front of electronic and digital screens?) Indeed, as the Jewish-German philosopher Walter Benjamin argued: contemporary humanity is fast approaching a consumer society of such mass-produced simulation and voyeurism that we may eventually forfeit all our powers of creativity and, instead, become spectators of our own self-destruction – and this without batting an eye. 'Mankind,' as Benjamin put it, 'which in Homer's time was an object of contemplation for the Olympian gods, now is one for itself.'[13]

But Beckett's apocalyptic fantasies may also serve to remind us that the ideological and religious fanaticism that governs so much of our world today, and is the cause of so much war and violence, stems from a refusal to experience the ambiguities and paradoxes of existence. It stems from a denial of the complexities that make up human reality. Beckett's own refusal of easy solutions to life's ultimate questions – life and death, theism and atheism, meaning and absurdity, self and other – may well be one of his most abiding gifts. Not forgetting, of course, the sheer fun, music, tenderness and unmistakeable mischievousness of the writing itself. A writing that never seems to come to an end, for as one of his unnamable narrators puts it, in words no doubt close to Beckett's all-too-human heart: 'I can't go on, I'll go on.' Here Beckett would seem to endorse the conviction of Paul Ricoeur in his classic study of narrative imagination, entitled *Time and Narrative*:

> Maybe we are the witnesses of a certain death of the art of narrating. [...] But maybe it is necessary, in spite of everything, to continue to believe that new forms of narrative, which we are not yet in a position to identify, are already in the process of being born, forms which would testify that the narrative function is capable of metamorphosis without actually dying. For we have no idea of what a culture would be in which one no longer knew what it means to narrate.[14]

In conclusion, then, might we not say that Beckett's undoing of storytelling itself takes the form of stories told, untold and retold. So that the very attempt to bring the story to an end is itself 'a search for a story to begin':

> [Y]ou must say words, as long as there are any, until they find me, until they say me [...] perhaps they have carried me to the threshold of my story, before the door that opens on my own story, that would surprise me, if it opens, it will be I, it will be the silence, where I am, I don't know, I'll never know, in the silence you don't know, you must go on, I can't go on, I'll go on.[15]

JOHN BANVILLE

Beckett's last words

O ne night in the early 1980s Samuel Beckett was having
dinner with his long-time English publisher, John
Calder, probably at *Les Iles Marquises* in Montparnasse,
Beckett's favourite restaurant at the time, or the beautifully
named bistro the *Closerie des Lilas*. During the course of the
meal Beckett diffidently announced to Calder that he had
something for him, and drew out of his shoulder bag a plastic
folder containing the typescript of *Ill Seen Ill Said*, the English
version of the short text – though long by Beckett's standards
– entitled *Mal vu mal dit*.

Calder was of course greatly excited at the prospect of a
new Beckett work, following closely as it did on *Company*, 'the
fable of one with you in the dark', a startlingly autobiographical
work, written, unusually, in English rather than French, which
the author had completed at the very end of the 1970s. Calder
put the typescript on the seat beside him and the two men
went on with their meal, finishing, no doubt, with a glass or
two of *marc*. When, some time later, Calder got back to his
hotel, he realised to his horror that he did not have the
typescript. In panic he telephoned the restaurant, but the folder
was not to be found. Could it have been thrown out? He

hurried back to the restaurant, which by now was closing, and persuaded the staff to let him look through the night's garbage. After a long and unpleasant search in bags of potato peelings and sodden bread and mussel shells he at last found the folder, smeared with food stains but with the typescript safe inside it – 'Thank God,' Calder said, 'that the folder was of plastic!'

Beckett was highly amused by the story, when Calder found the courage to tell it to him. How apt, after all, that a work by this connoisseur of detritus should have found its way accidentally into the rubbish bin. Yet when, some years after Beckett's death, I heard of the near-catastrophe – Beckett was notoriously lax in keeping copies of his typescripts – a shiver ran down my spine at the thought of the typescript going into the garbage truck, for *Ill Seen Ill Said*, short though it be, is one of the glories of late twentieth-century literature, or, indeed, of world literature of any period.

Beckett's artistic venture, from his first, exuberant volume of stories, *More Pricks Than Kicks*, published in 1934, to his last published writing, the poem 'what is the word', was un-equalled in its dedicated single-mindedness and unrelenting ideological rigour. That venture was always and only a struggle with and against language; as the narrator says in the wonderful fragment *From an Abandoned Work*: 'I love the word, words have been my only loves, not many.'[1] After the great trilogy of *Molloy*, *Malone Dies* and *The Unnamable*, and the last 'full-length' work, the novel *How It Is*, which appeared in 1961, the texts became shorter and shorter as the author pared down his material, until he achieved a kind of 'white-out' in such pieces as *Imagination Dead Imagine* and *All Strange Away*.

The effort, the concentration, the risk involved in this continuing throwing-out of literary ballast provided a rare and exemplary instance of artistic good faith. Throughout the 1960s and the 1970s Beckett's readers greeted each of the author's successively shorter and bleaker texts with a mixture of awe and apprehensiveness; it was like watching a great mathematician wielding an infinitesimal calculus, his equations approaching nearer and still nearer to the null point. Surely after *this*, we would say, the only possible advance will be into total silence at last. In those decades, however, the danger was not that he would go mute – Beckett's is a clamorous silence – but that the work would wither into sterility. Yet somehow he always found an escape route, no matter how strait the tunnel or how bleak the view at the end of it.

Beckett was first and last a prose writer, and regarded his plays as little more than footnotes to the novels – as late as 1966 he was still referring to the novel trilogy as '*toute mon oeuvre*'.[2] However, in the 1960s and the 1970s, Beckett turned repeatedly to the theatre, 'in search for a respite from the wasteland of prose',[3] as he put it. To his surprise and shy pleasure, it brought him somewhat out of himself, especially after the success of *Waiting for Godot*, which thrust him to world fame in the 1950s, and later when he made a number of genuine and lasting friendships among actors and directors. As the 1980s approached, however, he began to feel in earnest the fleeting of time, and yearned again for the solitude and concentration in which in the years after the war he had produced the trilogy – he spoke of that enterprise as 'the siege in the room' – and went off frequently to his modest country cottage at Ussy sur Marne to work on what would become the final masterpieces, *Company, Ill Seen Ill Said, Worstward Ho* and *Stirrings Still*.

Because of the lateness and comparative brevity of these pieces they are often regarded as mere shavings from the workbench, the ageing master's final whittlings as he succumbed to that silence which throughout his writing life had sung to him as the siren sang to Odysseus's sailors. This view is entirely mistaken. In his last decade Beckett found a new access of inspiration – 'Imagination at wit's end spreads its sad wings,' as the voice in *Ill Seen Ill Said* has it[4] – a final efflorescence which in these late texts would produce one of the most beautiful, profound and moving of literary testaments.

In Paris in the late 1920s and throughout the 1930s the young Beckett was much under the influence of James Joyce, for whom he did some secretarial work, and whose writings he championed, notably in his essay on what was to become

Finnegans Wake, 'Dante … Bruno. Vico … Joyce', in which he made the by now famous distinction: '[Joyce's] writing is not about something; *it is that something itself*,' a formulation that may apply more comfortably to Beckett's own work than to the encyclopaedic fabulations of Joyce. Later, Beckett sought artistically to strike the father dead (as all artists must do), speaking of Joyce's tendency towards 'omnipotence and omniscience', while he himself worked with 'impotence, ignorance'. This did not mean, he insisted, that in his own, new kind of art there would be no form, but only that there would be a new form, 'and this form will be of such a type that it admits the chaos and does not try to say that the chaos is really something else …'[5]

In an early essay on Proust, Beckett had insisted that the only progression possible for the modern artist is a *progression in depth*; the vast effort of inclusiveness of Balzac or Proust, or, indeed, of Joyce, must be abjured. In the first of three dialogues with the editor of *transition*, Georges Duthuit, published in 1949, Beckett speaks of 'an art … weary of puny exploits, weary of pretending to be able, of being able, of doing a little better the same old thing, of going a little further along a dreary road'. But what, the interviewer asked, is the alternative? Beckett's answer was simple, uncompromising and mordantly witty: 'The expression that there is nothing to express, nothing with which to express, nothing from which to express, no power to express, no desire to express, together with the obligation to express.'[6]

There are many readers still who find even the postwar trilogy of novels too daunting to attempt. Yet Beckett for all his seeming bleakness is a thoroughly entertaining writer. At one level the trilogy is a comic masterpiece, sparkling with wit and humour, and containing some splendid, blackly funny set-pieces. And the prose, of course, is never less than beautiful. Beckett's style is classical, poised, incantatory, yet one that will 'admit the chaos'. His models are the great masters of plain yet sonorous prose, such as Swift, Sir Thomas Browne, the English divines of the seventeenth and eighteenth centuries, and, above all, the translators of the King James Bible. The last century's other master of English, James Joyce, was essentially a Catholic writer; his work bristles with imagery from the Catholic liturgy, and many of the effects it seeks for depend on typographical presentation: these texts – even *Finnegans Wake*, for all its vaunted musicality – were written to be *seen on the page*. On this level Beckett is very much an Anglo-Irish Protestant, his language resonating – 'like a verse of Isaiah, or of Jeremiah', as his creature Molloy says[7] – as if delivered from the pulpit of a bare, three-quarters-empty church.

It will perhaps seem paradoxical to suggest that Beckett even in his late work is in many ways a traditional novelist, but I believe that he is. His characters, though few in type, are strongly drawn, and certainly memorable, and his plots are interesting (consider in the novel *Molloy* Moran's vain pursuit of its eponymous protagonist, or the drama of the nameless narrator's agonised journey through the mud in *How It Is*); his fictions, even the briefest of them, have beginnings, middles and ends; and practically all of them have a 'twist in the tail' – Beckett, after all, was an avid reader of American and French thrillers. In *Molloy*, Moran begins his narrative thus: 'It is midnight. The rain is beating on the windows.' At the very end, after much journeying and many vicissitudes, he tells how he returned home to find himself mysteriously estranged from all that he once knew as familiar: 'Then I went back into the house and wrote, It is midnight. The rain is beating on the windows. It was not midnight. It was not raining.'[8] And with that, the entire book collapses like a house of cards.

Beckett's themes are simple and universal. As the critic S.E. Gontarski puts it: 'Childhood memories, adolescent un-happiness, fears of mortality, wasted opportunities, familial and cultural alienation, memories of suicidal sweethearts: these are the elements Beckett's art needs and needs to undo as he struggles to make universal art out of personal neurosis.'[9] In other words, what he is dealing with is no less or more than life, the commonplace thing itself, in all its disorder, hilarity, ecstasy and pain.

But if the content of Beckett's work is conventional, its methods are not. His fictions advance by a kind of reverse progression, denying and consuming themselves as they go; as Wolfgang Iser puts it: 'The Beckett reader is continually being confronted by statements that are no longer valid. But as the negated statements remain present in his mind, so the indeterminacy of the text increases, thus increasing the pressure on the reader to find out what is being withheld from him.'[10] This is what Gontarski calls 'the intent of undoing'.

Of course, Beckett is not the first artist to 'affirm by negation'. Some of the greatest writers of this century, from Rilke and Hofmannsthal to Celan and Thomas Bernhard, have produced work that derives its power and pathos from the negative, from all that is absent from it. Negation is not nihilism. The statement of an absence implies a presence elsewhere. (Oh yes, Kafka remarked to his friend Max Brod, there is hope, plenty of hope – but not for us.) This is not to claim Beckett as a covert champion of an outmoded humanism, yet neither is he a harbinger of The End, as posthumanist commentators such as Theodor Adorno have all too often and too fiercely affirmed him to be. The essence of art is that like a river in flood it flows around obstacles and finds new ways of progressing. One of Beckett's favourite lines from Shakespeare is the observation by Edgar in *King Lear* that 'the worst is not/So long as we can say "This is the worst".'[11] And *The Unnamable*'s last words are, famously: 'I can't go on. I'll go on.' *Worstward Ho* ends thus:

Nohow less. Nohow worse. Nohow naught. Nohow on.

Said nohow on.[12]

The point being, in my reading of it, that to have *said* nohow on is already to have found a way forward.

It is meaningless to describe Beckett, as he is often described, as a pessimist. His work is neither pessimistic nor optimistic; like all true art, it simply *is*. By its very existence it affirms, but affirmation is not always positive. A story is told of

Beckett walking in London with friends one fine summer morning and remarking on the splendours of the day. One of the friends agrees, and suggests that on such a day it is good to be alive, to which Beckett replies: 'Well, I wouldn't go so far as that!'[13] Yet Beckett's narrators, even in their worst extremes of anguish, profess a deep fondness for the world. 'Great love in my heart too for all things still and rooted,' says the voice in *From an Abandoned Work*, and goes on:

Oh I know I too shall cease and be as when I was not yet, only all over instead of in store, that makes me happy, often now my murmur falters and dies and I weep for happiness as I go along and for love of this old earth that has carried me so long and whose uncomplainingness will soon be mine. Just under the surface I shall be, all together at first, then separate and drift, through all the earth and perhaps in the end through a cliff into the sea, something of me.[14]

When we consider these and countless other such tender passages in the work of his middle period, we realise that the fictions of the 1980s represent no real change of direction but merely an intensification of concerns that were always present but repressed in favour of the ferocity of Beckett's sensibility in the immediate postwar period.

'A voice comes to one in the dark. Imagine.' Thus begins *Company*.[15] It is, I feel, the least successful of the four final works. The conjunction is uneasy between the solitary hearer lying in blackness and the bright images called up for him from childhood; the 'intent of undoing' is too apparent. Also, Beckett comes perilously close here to sentimentality. The images of the little boy holding his mother's hand, or sitting with his father in the summerhouse, or trying to make a pet of a hedgehog, have a touch almost of Enid Blyton about them. Yet *Company* contains some of late Beckett's sparest and most supple prose, and in the end the old, harsh honesty is there, as this 'devised deviser devising it all for company' comes clean at last:

You now on your back in the dark shall not rise to your arse again to clasp your legs in your arms and bow down your head till it can bow down no farther. But with face upturned for good labour in vain at your fable. Till finally you hear how words are coming to an end. With every inane word a little nearer to the last. And how the fable too. The fable of one with you in the dark. The fable of one fabling of one with you in the dark. And how better in the end labour lost and silence. And you as you always were.

Alone.[16]

While *Company* and *Worstward Ho* may be described as autobiographical in the broadest sense, *Ill Seen Ill Said*, the finest of these late works, is narrated in the third person, and has as its central figure a dying old woman, alone amid the snows at lambing time and watched over by a mysterious Twelve who ring the clearing where her cabin stands. It is profound and moving, an extended poetic meditation on eschatology; these last things shake the heart:

> Winter evening in the pastures. The snow has ceased. Her steps so light they barely leave a trace. Have barely left having ceased. Just enough to be still visible. Adrift the snow. Whither in her head while her feet stray thus? Hither and thither too? Or unswerving to the mirage? And where when she halts? The eye discerns afar a kind of stain. Finally the steep roof whence part of the fresh fall has slid. Under the low lowering sky the north is lost. Obliterated by the snow the twelve are there.[17]

Though all the movement of the work is towards death, the end is strangely joyful: 'One moment more. One last. Grace to breathe that void. Know happiness.'[18] Lawrence Graver has remarked, somewhat menacingly, that 'speculation about the biographical significance' of the piece cannot go far 'until scholarly studies tell us a good deal more than we now know about the fiery relationship of May Beckett and her son', yet he does declare 'how extraordinary it is that the mother-haunted *Ill Seen Ill Said* should be – for all its provisionality and anguish – arguably the most conclusive and serene of the old master's works'.[19] Certainly it is the most tender. Beckett here seems to hover over the old woman who is his creation with all of a benign creator's care and helpless sorrow. Once even he lets himself appear directly in the text: 'She shows herself only to her own. But she has no own. Yes yes she has one. And who has her.'[20]

Serene is not a word one would apply to *Worstward Ho*. This is a difficult, spiky work, built up arduously out of short, percussive sentences, as if the bearer of some terrible news had come stumbling to a halt before us and begun to stammer out his message: 'On. Say on. Be said on. Somehow on. Till nohow on. Said nohow on.'[21] The entire piece is contained *in ovo* in this opening. Over the following couple of dozen pages the breathless speaker strives, mostly in vain, to unravel the sense of things. It is a frightful task. 'Less worse then? Enough. A pox on void. Unmoreable unlessable unworseable evermost almost void.'[22] And yet despite the difficulties there are pleasures to be derived. The piece is strangely bracing in its energy and pace, and we are gripped by a sense that all this that is going on – whatever it may be – does *matter*. 'The words [...] How almost true they sometimes almost ring!'[23] As always in Beckett, there is consolation to be derived from the right articulation of even the deepest sorrow.

What do they *mean*, these strange, fraught, desperate fictions? Are we to take any meaning from them? Are they 'about' something, or are they that something itself? There are many explicitly religious references, especially in *Ill Seen Ill Said*, which speaks of one of the old woman's gestures being 'full of grace',[24] and of a nail in the wall 'All set to serve again. Like unto its glorious ancestors. At the place of the skull. One April afternoon. Deposition done.'[25] Where such references are concerned, however, it would be well to remember Beckett's remarks about his use in *Waiting for Godot* of the anecdote of the two thieves crucified with Christ, one of whom was saved and the other damned: it was not the theological aspect that interested him, he said – he merely *liked the shape of the idea*.

I believe that all of Beckett's work, from the fumblings of the hapless Belacqua in *More Pricks than Kicks* to the final, benighted groping for speech in the poem 'what is the word', is first and foremost a critique of language, of the deceptiveness of words, and of our illusions about what we can express and the value of expression, and that it was his genius to produce out of such an enterprise these moving, disconsolate and scrupulously crafted works.

Beckett is an exemplary figure. He presents for the writers who came after him a model of probity and tenacity which is a secret source of strength in an age when literature itself seems under threat. He refused to take part in the cult of personality, maintaining an admirable reticence in the face of a gossip-obsessed world. He lived, he wrote; the rest, in the wise words of Henry James, is the madness of art. When I think of him I always recall his description in *Malone Dies* of young Sapo watching the flight of the hawk, 'fascinated by such extremes of need, of pride, of patience and solitude'.[26]

BARRY
McGOVERN

Beckett and the radio voice

'A voice comes to one in the dark. Imagine.'[1] These opening words of Samuel Beckett's prose text *Company*
encapsulate the situation of the radio voice. It is a
world where sound and silence are the only coordinates. It is
the world of the imagination.

In June 1956 the BBC invited Beckett to write a play for
radio. Beckett would not accept a commission but did agree to
try to write something. That summer in a letter to his American
publisher, Barney Rosset of Grove Press, he said: 'Haven't made
much progress with Third Programme script. Not interested.'[2]
A month later it was finished. It was directed by Donald
McWhinnie and broadcast on 13 January 1957. *All That Fall*
was Beckett's first play written in English, his mother tongue.

After *All That Fall* there followed other plays written for
radio: *Embers*, first broadcast in 1959; *Words and Music* in 1962;
Cascando in 1963; and the two *Rough[s] for Radio* written in the
early sixties – the second one first broadcast in 1976. (The first
Rough, at Beckett's request, is not for production, the author
feeling that *Cascando* had overtaken it, so to speak.) There is
also, from 1960, *The Old Tune*, an adaptation of Robert Pinget's
La Manivelle into wonderful Dublinese. Cream and Gorman
are two O'Casey-like characters reminiscing on a park bench.

Radio was a particularly suitable medium for Beckett. Apart from the plays written specifically for the medium, much of his prose and poetry has been broadcast. He himself was involved with a number of broadcasts of his work in the 1960s and 1970s. And it was hearing Patrick Magee reading from the novel *Molloy* in December 1957 on the BBC Third Programme that sowed the seed for *Magee Monologue* which became *Krapp's Last Tape*, one of his finest achievements.

As well as the radio plays much of the later shorter prose had early outings on radio: *Imagination Dead Imagine, Lessness, The Lost Ones, First Love, Company, Ill Seen Ill Said, Worstward Ho* and *Stirrings Still*, among others. The poetry, too, perhaps the least-known part of his writing, has had radio programmes devoted to it.

One of the reasons why radio is so suitable for Beckett's work is that in Beckett, especially from the great middle period on, the central medium for his characters is storytelling. 'Stories, stories, years and years of stories, till the need came on me, for someone, to be with me, anyone, a stranger, to talk to, imagine he hears me, years of that …'[3] Thus, Henry in *Embers*. Or Hamm in *Endgame*: 'Enough of that, it's story time, where was I?' (116). And later: 'Perhaps I could go on with my story, end it and begin another' (126). In the four great stories, or novellas, from 1946, *The End, The Expelled, First Love* and *The Calmative*, we have the first-person narrator telling stories. This unnamed character (or characters – it doesn't matter, it's the same voice) is very much the prototype of Molloy, Moran, Malone, the narrator of *The Unnamable*, the protagonist of *How It Is* and the other moribunds that abound in Beckett's later fiction. They are all ultimately looking for silence, for the end of words, for peace from words. But the only way they can find that end of words is by using words. As the narrator of *From an Abandoned Work* says: 'words have been my only loves, not many'.[4] Perhaps the narrator of *The Unnamable* sums it up best: 'This voice that speaks […] It issues from me, it fills me, it clamours against my walls, it is not mine, I can't stop it, I can't prevent it, from tearing me, racking me, assailing me. It is not mine, I have none, I have no voice and must speak, that is all I know.'[5]

So many of Beckett's characters suffer not only from a *need* to speak but an *obligation* to speak. They are, in their own way, artists. Beckett himself, in one of his *Three Dialogues* with Georges Duthuit, speaks of an art in which 'there is nothing to express, nothing with which to express, nothing from which to express, no power to express, no desire to express, together with the obligation to express'.[6] 'I cannot be silent', says the narrator of *The Unnamable* very early on in that novel. And, a little later, he wonders about the ultimate Beckett fantasy: 'If I could speak and yet say nothing, really nothing?'[7]

If we consider the nature of the voice in Beckett's plays written specifically for radio, we may do worse than look at them chronologically. In a letter to his friend Nancy Cunard on 5 July 1956 he said: 'Never thought about a radio play technique, but in the dead of t'other night got a nicely gruesome idea full of cartwheels and dragging feet and puffing and panting which may or may not lead to something.'[8] The something it led to was *All That Fall* – originally titled *Lovely Day for the Races*. The title is taken from Psalm 145, verse 14: 'The Lord upholdeth all that fall and raiseth up all those that be bowed down.' He wrote the play very quickly and it has very few drafts. The holograph is dated 'Ussy September 1956.' It was sent to the BBC on 27 September. The play is set in the village of Boghill – for which read Foxrock, Co. Dublin – some time in the 1930s. Maddy Rooney (*née* Dunne), a fat woman in her seventies, is on her way to the local railway station to meet her blind and elderly husband Dan who is on his way home from his office. She passes a 'ruinous old house'[9] where a lonely woman plays a record of Schubert's *Death and the Maiden*. (We are not told whether it is the song or the string quartet.) The themes of death and maidenhood are central to the play. She meets a number of men on her way to the station all involved with progressively faster forms of transport: Christy with his hinny and dung-cart; Mr Tyler with his bicycle; Mr Slocum (who gives her a lift) with his car. At the station she is helped out of Mr Slocum's car by Tommy, the station porter, and up the steps by Miss Fitt. The train is late and Mr Barrell, the station master, does not know why. After a delay of some fifteen minutes the train arrives and Dan finally appears. The second half of the play is taken up with their homeward journey on foot. Maddy tries to find out what has delayed the train but Dan prevaricates and digresses. He talks about life in his office and the horrors of domesticity; Maddy speaks of her lack of children and other matters. Eventually a boy arrives (something familiar here), Jerry, with a ball-like object which Mr Barrell said belonged to Dan. When Maddy asks what kept the train late, Jerry replies: 'It was a little child fell out of the carriage, Ma'am. [*Pause.*] On to the line, Ma'am. [*Pause.*] Under the wheels, Ma'am' (199). The Rooneys then trudge homeward through a tempest of wind and rain.

Though the story or plot of *All That Fall*, such as it is, is in the form of a mystery about what happened on the train, the interesting thing about the play is the feeling of decay and the sense of falling that is built up through the various encounters Maddy has with the other characters and the distinctive and indeed suggestive overtones of each person's speech. This is also prevalent in the return journey home with Maddy and Dan on their own. Echoes of the voices from the middle period fiction abound, for example: 'How can I go on, I cannot' (174); 'It is suicide to be abroad. But what is it to be at home, Mr Tyler, what is it to be at home? A lingering dissolution.' Likewise Mr Tyler: 'I was merely cursing, under my breath, God and man, under my breath, and the wet Saturday afternoon of my conception' (175). But perhaps the Beckettian voice is most obviously in evidence in Dan Rooney's speech about his thoughts on work and home as he travelled homeward in the train. The misanthrope and miser tells his patient wife that he worked out his expenses and found he would be better off in bed. 'Business, old man, I said, retire from business, it has retired from you. [...] On the other hand, I said, there are the horrors of home life, the dusting, sweeping, airing, scrubbing, waxing, waning, washing, mangling, drying, mowing, clipping, raking, rolling, scuffling, shovelling, grinding, tearing, pounding, banging and slamming.' He begins to think also of the noisy children in the vicinity known to him only at weekends and wonders in horror what the noise must be like on other days. 'And I fell to thinking of my silent, backstreet, basement office, with its obliterated plate, rest-couch and velvet hangings, and what it means to be buried there alive, if only from ten to five, with convenient to the one hand a bottle of light pale ale and to the other a long ice-cold fillet of hake. Nothing, I said, not even fully certified death, can ever take the place of that' (193-94).

This voice is very reminiscent of Moran in the novel *Molloy*. It is a voice that has, perhaps, its origins in the kind of people who would have been friends and neighbours of Beckett and his parents in early twentieth-century Foxrock. But it is unique in Beckett's radio plays in its naturalistic roots. His next play for radio was to be a much stiffer proposition.

The voice in *Embers*, written in 1959, is quite different. Originally titled *Ebb*, partly because of the importance of the sound of the sea, this play is more of an interior monologue than *All That Fall*. Basically the play consists of two monologues by Henry interspersed with a scene with Henry's wife Ada whose voice is 'low' and 'remote' throughout (257), perhaps signifying that her presence is only in Henry's head. This scene in turn is interspersed with two very short scenes featuring their daughter Addie having a music lesson and a riding lesson. These scenes were added to the text by Beckett as an afterthought. The monologues in turn are interspersed with Henry's story about Bolton and Holloway.

Henry in his monologue conjures up his father and his wife Ada. His father has probably committed suicide by drowning. Henry is obsessed with ending it all, like so many of Beckett's characters. He rails against life; against his dead father who called him 'a washout' (256); wishes his mother had aborted him; wishes he'd never had his daughter Addie; is sardonically insulting to his wife Ada. As she says to him with reference to his father: 'You wore him out living and now you are wearing him out dead' (262). Sounds promising so far, no? But as always in Beckett a bare description or synopsis never suffices. It's not the 'what', it's the 'how' that matters. *Embers* is a very funny play, like all Beckett's work. But the humour is very black and very sardonic. Unless the actor playing Henry has a feel for the irony and sarcasm needed the play will not come across properly. The darkness of the piece can only register if the humour leavens it.

Henry's story is 'about an old fellow called Bolton' (254), and a doctor called Holloway. Bolton is an 'old man in great trouble' (255) who has summoned Holloway to his house on a bright winter's night. It seems that Holloway wants to give Bolton his usual injection which may be a pain-killer but Bolton wants more than that – perhaps a lethal dose. These story sections are exquisitely written and very evocative. Henry tells the tragic story in three sections in the play. But he can't finish it. The second attempt begins: 'Try again.' And it ends: 'No good. [*Pause.*] Can't do it' (255–6). The last, graphic section likewise ends 'no good. [*Pause.*] No good' (264). Like most of Beckett's characters' stories, it is unfinished. Remember the last word of Lucky's monologue in *Waiting for Godot* – 'unfinished' (43). And the first words of *Endgame*: 'Finished, it's finished, nearly finished, it must be nearly finished' (92). But at the end of the play Clov is still standing at the door. He has not left. It is unfinished.

There are probably more pauses in *Embers* than in any other play by Beckett. Two hundred and twenty-eight according to Clas Zilliacus in his monumental study of the radio and TV plays *Beckett and Broadcasting*. The voice of Henry has to balance these two aural modes, sound and silence. It is a delicate balance.

Let me now turn briefly to the two plays *Rough for Radio 1* and *Rough for Radio 2*, written sometime in the early 1960s. Their date of composition is problematic but it seems that *Rough for Radio 1* (or *Esquisse Radiophonique* as it was titled in the original French) was written after *Words and Music* and before *Cascando*.

Rough for Radio 1 involves a man who is obsessed with voice and music – so much so that he needs medical attention. 'He' is visited by an unnamed woman, 'She', to listen to the faint sounds of both Voice and Music, first separately, then together. 'He' tells her that both Voice and Music have become needs. 'She' does not seem very interested and leaves him to his needs. After she leaves he tries twice to get the doctor on the phone. Eventually he gets to speak to him. Meanwhile, the voice and music, formally 'not together' (though sounding at the same time), are now 'Like one!' (268–70). They are, he agitatedly tells the doctor, 'ENDING' and 'they're together ... TOGETHER [...] like ... [*Hesitation.*] ... one' (270–1). 'He' is clearly distressed and doesn't take much comfort when the doctor tells him that last gasps are all alike. Echoes of Pozzo here. The doctor hangs up but the secretary rings back to say the doctor has been delayed by two confinements (first gasps?), one a breech birth, and will not be able to make it until 'tomorrow noon'. 'Tomorrow ... noon ...' 'He' whispers after a long pause and the play ends. Late sparks from *Embers*, perhaps. The voice of 'He' in the second half of this short play is urgent, seeking, fretful and ultimately resigned. It is very similar to the questing voice uttered in short panting phrases I shall discuss later in this lecture.

Rough for Radio 2 (or *Pochade Radiophonique* in the original French) was probably written in the early 1960s but is almost impossible to date with accuracy. It concerns the efforts of three characters, Animator, Stenographer and Dick, to elicit by torture some sort of utterance from a fourth character, Fox, which will finally set them free. It is similar in some ways to the situation in an unpublished story from the early 1950s *On le tortura bien* ('He was well tortured'). It is also reminiscent of parts of *How It Is* and *What Where*. In this cryptic but witty play it is the voice of Fox which is the quintessential Beckett radio voice. This character is some kind of rodent-like human creature who is constantly burrowing and seeking among stones and tunnels. He seems to have a twin brother inside him. This surreal character speaks in short bursts rather like the narrator in the latter stages of *The Unnamable*. The stenographer takes down everything Fox says but it is not enough for the other characters' liberty. Animator insists on inserting words never said by Fox despite Stenographer's objection. In the end it comes down to a question of bending the truth to get relief.

Words and Music and *Cascando*, both written in 1961, are different creatures altogether. These plays have to do with the act of creation. Both use words and music. In the play *Words and Music* there is a character called Croak (never named orally) who has two minions, Words and Music. Words is called Joe and Music, Bob. Words rehearses a speech on the theme of sloth. When Croak appears muttering about a face on the stairs, in the tower, and gives Words the subject 'love', Words patters out a passage on the theme of love similar to the one he rehearsed on sloth. Croak stops him with a thump of his club on the ground and asks Music to express himself on the subject of love (288). Words cannot bear Music's expressiveness and he groans. Croak pleads with his 'comforts', his 'balms' to 'be friends' (291). When Words, now asked to speak on the subject 'age', begins a poem, Croak urges Words and Music to express themselves together, Words singing softly a poem on age and lost love. Croak then murmurs repeatedly 'the face' and, later, 'Lily' (292). But, after Words' rhetoric is too much for him, he departs, leaving Words and Music together. Words implores Music to play and, at the end, sighs, leaving us perhaps with the impression that Music has triumphed.

The dominant voice in this play is undoubtedly Words who, like Lucky in *Waiting for Godot*, patters out formulaic definitions of sloth, love and 'the face', eventually changing to the two songs which dominate the second half of this curious play. They bear quoting, first on age:

> Age is when to a man
> Huddled o'er the ingle
> Shivering for the hag
> To put the pan in the bed

And bring the toddy
She comes in the ashes
Who loved could not be won
Or won not loved
Or some other trouble
Comes in the ashes
Like in that old light
The face in the ashes
That old starlight
On the earth again. (291)

And the second, describing the very essence of creativity:

Then down a little way
Through the trash
Towards where
All dark no begging
No giving no words
No sense no need
Through the scum
Down a little way
To whence one glimpse
Of that wellhead. (293–4)

The actors' voices must carry with them, on the one hand, the eternal anguish of creativity and, on the other, its mystery.

Cascando, though similar, is in some respects quite different. Beckett once said that the play is 'about the character called Woburn' (Maunu in the original French), 'who never appears'.[10] But of course it is about far more than that. It too is concerned with the act of creation. A character called Opener opens two channels, so to speak; one being the character called Voice and the other, Music. Sometimes Voice speaks on his own (and it *is* a male voice) and sometimes Music plays on its own. At other times they sound together. The play has some similarities to Beckett's novel *The Unnamable* in that there is a panting voice seeking silence. If silence is the quarry, then Woburn is the personification of that quarry. Just as the narrator of *The Unnamable* concludes that novel with the words 'you must go on, I can't go on, I'll go on',[11] so Opener at one stage says, 'I'm afraid to open. But I must open. So I open' (*CDW* 302). In a way Voice is an aspect of Opener. In early drafts Voice was called Voice Two – Opener being Voice One. Voice Two was sub-divided into self and story. Opener at times says things like 'They say, it's in his head. No' (299). Or, 'They say, That is not his life, he does not live on that. They don't see me, they don't see what my life is, they don't see what I live on, and they say, That is not his life, he does not live on that. [*Pause.*] I have lived on it . . . till I'm old. Old enough. Listen' (300). And again Voice continues his story about the quest for Woburn. In a French typescript the direction for Voice's delivery is *débit rapide, haletant* (*rapid delivery, panting*). In the published texts it is *bas, haletant* (*low, panting*). The style and content of the writing has much in common with Fox in *Rough for Radio 2* and Mouth in the stage play *Not I* and, as mentioned, the narrator's voice in the latter part of *The Unnamable*. It is a matter of rhythm, phrasing and the shifts between them. Compare the following four excerpts, in order of composition. The first example is from the end of *The Unnamable*:

> perhaps it's a dream, all a dream, that would surprise me, I'll wake, in the silence, and never sleep again, it will be I, or dream, dream again, dream of a silence, a dream silence, full of murmurs, I don't know, that's all words, never wake, all words, there's nothing else, you must go on, that's all I know, they're going to stop, I know that well, I can feel it, they're going to abandon me, it will be the silence, for a moment, a good few moments, or it will be mine, the lasting one, that didn't last, that still lasts, it will be I, you must go on, I can't go on, you must go on, I'll go on, you must say words, as long as they are any, until they find me, until they say me, strange pain, strange sin, you must go on, perhaps it's done already, perhaps they have said me already, perhaps they have carried me to the threshold of my story, before the door that opens on my story, that would surprise me, if it opens, it will be I, it will be the silence, where I am, I don't know, I'll never know, in the silence you don't know, you must go on, I can't go on, I'll go on.[12]

Now, from the beginning of *Cascando*:

VOICE: [*Low, panting.*] – story ... if you could finish it ... you could rest ... sleep ... not before ... oh I know ... the ones I've finished ... thousands and one ... all I ever did ... in my life ... with my life ... saying to myself ... finish this one ... it's the right one ... then rest ... sleep ... no more stories ... no more words ... and finished it ... and not the right one ... couldn't rest ... straight away another ... to begin ... to finish ... saying to myself ... finish this one ... then rest ... this time ... it's the right one ... this time ... you have it ... and finished it ... and not the right one ...[13]

Now, from *Rough for Radio 2*, Fox begins: 'Ah yes, that for sure, live I did, no denying, all stones all sides--', resumes, 'walls no further – ' (*CDW* 277) and launches into a long speech, punctuated by Animator's 'thumps on his desk with a cylindrical ruler':

That for sure, no further, and there gaze, all the way up, all the way down, slow gaze, age upon age, up again, down again, little lichens of my little [14] span, living dead in the stones, and there took to the tunnels. [*Silence. Ruler.*] Oceans too, that too, no denying, I drew near down the tunnels, blue above, blue ahead, that for sure, and there too, no further, ways end, all ends and farewell, farewell and fall, farewell seasons, till I fare again. [Silence. Ruler.] Farewell. (*CDW* 279)

Finally, Mouth from the opening of *Not I*:

.... out ... into this world ... this world ... tiny little thing ... before its time ... in a godfor– ... what? ... girl? ... yes ... tiny little girl ... into this ... out into this ... before her time ... godforsaken hole called ... called ... no matter ... parents unknown ... unheard of ... he having vanished ... thin air ... no sooner buttoned up his breeches ... she similarly .. eight months later ... almost to the tick ... so no love ... spared that ... so such love as normally vented on the ... speechless infant ... in the home ... no ... nor indeed for that matter any of any kind ... no love of any kind ... at any subsequent stage ... so typical affair ... nothing of any note till coming up to sixty when– ... what? ... seventy? ... good God! ... coming up to seventy ... wandering in a field ... looking aimlessly for cowslips ... to make a ball ... a few steps then stop ... stare into space ... then on ... a few more ... stop and stare again ... so on ... drifting around ... when suddenly ... gradually ... all went out ... all that early April morning light ... and she found herself in the– ... what? ... who? ... no! ... she! (376–7)

We can see from these excerpts an example of one type of Beckettian voice; a harried, rushing, nervy voice – phrased in short panting bursts. The narrator of *The Unnamable* – searching for silence and an end to words; Voice in *Cascando* – looking for rest and sleep and an end to stories and words; Fox (with overtones of *Vox*, latin for voice) in *Rough for Radio 2* – tortured into speech and forced to utter. His story may lead to final peace for the other characters. Finally, in *Not I*, Mouth tells a story of abandonment and disablement, hearing a voice which corrects her from time to time. But one correction she never accepts. It is 'not I', she screams, but 'she'. An other. Mouth will never accept that she herself is the one she is obsessively talking about.

I have chosen to give examples from *Not I* and *The Unnamable*, even though they are not radio plays (indeed *The Unnamable* is not a play), because the voice in these works is, in a way, a radio voice. It is *'coming out of the dark'* to quote Beckett from 1957 when refusing permission for a staging of *All That Fall*. He said, 'I am absolutely opposed to any form of adaptation with a view to its conversion into "theatre". It is no more theatre than *End-Game* [sic] is radio and to "act" it is to kill it. Even the reduced visual dimension it will receive from the simplest and most static of readings [...] will be destructive of whatever quality it may have and which depends on the whole thing's *coming out of the dark*.'[15]

Beckett's voices come out of the dark, come into light and go back to the dark: 'the light gleams an instant, then it's night once more' (*CDW* 83). Hamm in *Endgame* and Dan Rooney in *All That Fall*, being blind, are in the dark – literally. As are the three characters in *Play* until interrogated by light. 'Yes, strange, darkness best,' begins Woman 1 in *Play* (307); and later, 'Silence and darkness were all I craved' (316). The radio voice is a refinement of these voices. It is an insistent, probing voice. Like railway tracks that fade into the distance seemingly approaching one another but never quite meeting, it is constantly narrowing down to an essence which is ultimately unattainable because ultimately unknowable. All the dead voices become one vital voice in its quest for 'the one true end to time and grief and self',[16] the silence that follows 'the unanswerable clamour'.[17]

KATHARINE WORTH

Beckett on the world stage

T he Irishman who grew up in Dublin and spoke English with an Irish lilt to the end of his days took his first step as playwright on to the world stage in 1953 with a play written in French and performed by French actors at the Théâtre de Babylone, Paris. Two years later, Beckett's *En attendant Godot* in its English version, *Waiting for Godot*, was being played by English actors at the Arts Theatre, London. The tale of two cities then took a curious turn, as if to hint at the future spread of Beckett's art on the world stage, when his next play, *Fin de partie*, temporarily unable to find a stage in Paris, opened in London in 1957 at the Royal Court Theatre. A testing experience for those English members of the audience less than fluent in French and confronted with a play unlike anything ever seen before, in either language. Beckett memorably described the experience as 'rather grim, like playing to mahogany, or rather teak'. Within a month the production had found the desired home in Paris at the Studio des Champs-Elysées, no doubt to the relief of the French cast.

But the Royal Court Theatre had helped to place London firmly in the Beckettian landscape with its launching of this play in French. The theatre received a handsome acknowledgment of that support when in 1958 they were given the first staging of *Krapp's Last Tape*, with the solo role thrillingly played by Patrick Magee. The Anglo-French détente stimulated by these happenings had a fine climax in that same year when the Royal Court boldly took its audiences back to *Fin de partie*, now in its English version as *Endgame*, with Clov played by another Irish actor who was to be dear to Beckett, Jack MacGowran. And in 1976, two new plays, *That Time* and *Footfalls*, were both given their premières in this theatre. Beckett was faithful to his friends.

None of this would have been possible, of course, without Beckett's ability and desire to move from one language to another within a variety of genres, including plays. As Ann Beer has noted, Beckett's bilingualism was not forced upon him but was a voluntary drive related to his 'constant ability to see artistic forms afresh'.[1] His commitment to self-translation was remarkable. Ruby Cohn conveyed the strangeness of it when she remarked that he could never predict whether the voice that came to him in the dark would speak English or French.[2] That there was sometimes a sense of burdensome necessity about the ingrained habit of self-translation was an impression I received in conversation with him once, when he was engaged in just such a task. But he wanted and needed to do it all the same.

Ireland entered the Beckettian scene soon after the première of *Godot* in London with a production of the play in Dublin. In 1968, at the Peacock Theatre, the première was held of *Come and Go* in English (as *Kommen und Gehen* it had been produced two years earlier in Berlin). The outstanding Irish contribution to Beckett's spreading fame in these years was probably the distinctive flavour brought to his first plays by his Irish actors. In 1991, however, the Gate Theatre Dublin realised the ambitious plan of their artistic director, Michael Colgan, presenting nineteen of the plays there and in 1999 constructing an augmented programme which went from Dublin to the Barbican Theatre, London. The many visitors from abroad who swelled the audiences on these occasions confirmed the impression that had been building up from the earliest days, of a unique drama destined for a world stage. Another massive assertion of Beckett's great reach as a playwright followed with the filming of the dramatic oeuvre initiated by Michael Colgan, and carried through by an Anglo-Irish combination of broadcasting companies, RTÉ and Channel 4.

The transmission of the plays across the world was hastened by the early, energetic entrance of America to the Beckettian scene. The first American production of *Godot* directed by Alan Schneider opened at the Coconut Theatre, Miami, in 1956, with the celebrated comic Bert Lahr playing Estragon (initially without much grasp on the part). But it was a production of 1957 by Herbert Blau with the Actors Company in San Francisco that demonstrated, as David Bradby has commented, the play's power to 'reach out to people of all cultures and backgrounds'.[3] Then in 1961 *Happy Days*, the third of the great trio at the start of Beckett's oeuvre and the only one of them to be first written and performed in English, opened at the Cherry Lane Theatre, New York.

One outcome of the close connection with American directors such as Schneider was Beckett's move into a new medium, film, and his first – and only – visit to the U.S.A. The process of making a film (with Bert Lahr at the centre) had for him the kind of interest in a genre not tried before which is hinted at by his entitling it, simply, *Film*. Made in 1964 and shown at the New York Film Festival in 1967, it did not satisfy him but neither did it lessen his interest in the possibilities of the screen (as he was to show in his plays for television). And many American premières of his stage plays were to follow; from *Not I* in 1972 to the last of the plays, *What Where*, in 1983, both in New York.

Well before then another European country, Germany, had made a spectacular public entrance to the Beckett scene with a production of the play provocatively entitled *Play* – or, *Spiel*, its name for the première at the Ulmer Theater, Ulm-Donau, in 1963. The text (in German translation by Erika and Elmer Tophoven) was published that same year. It was not till the following year that *Play* in English was first performed and published in London. Such, already, was the openness to Europe of Beckett's theatre art. It was also the start of a continuous connection on his part with German theatre. His own production of *Godot* with the Schiller Theater in 1975 was a striking demonstration of the new currents of creativity released by these collaborations. To see this when it came to London in 1976, even for those who had experienced other strong productions, was to have a sense of coming closer to the power mysteriously inherent in the play. Beckett described that power as something he himself didn't quite understand, when attempting to cheer Barney Rossett about the unsatisfactory production at the Coconut Grove. The play would survive, he assured him; it 'worms its way into people whether they like it or not'.[4]

No doubt that would happen in the end for some who initially disliked the play at its English première in 1955, directed by the young Peter Hall. Though Hall now criticises his production as an apprentice work, he must surely know that it gave the audience the sense of an experience totally new, such as Keats had on first reading Homer in translation and feeling 'like some watcher of the skies/When a new planet swims into his ken'. Just such an experience came about again, in fuller measure, through Beckett's own production of the German text in 1975. From the German connection also sprang two memorable plays for television, the brief, visionary *Nacht und Träume* and the engrossing *Quad*, with its hypnotically shuffling dancers moving in silence about their set courses.

The plays travelled very quickly on the world stage, styles of production often changing markedly with the decades and place of performance. The process can be illustrated from a European country, Greece, and an Asian one, Japan. Both came early to the Beckettian scene with productions in 1960.

In Greece the first production was of *Endgame* at the Pocket Theatre of Kollatos and Rialdi. It was a natural choice, the part of Nell in the première of the play as *Fin de partie* having been performed by Christina Tsingou, a French-speaking actress of Greek origin, at the time resident in Paris and personally acquainted with Beckett. This first part for a woman on Beckett's stage gave her, as Nell, a tightly limited role (literally so, enclosed as she was in an urn). But it gave her great chances which she later built on when spreading awareness of Beckett's oeuvre in Greece. Hers was a different experience from that of Billie Whitelaw who has vividly described the total commitment to performance demanded of her by Beckett as playwright/director.[5] The arduous rehearsing with him demanded a commitment that was to make her the un-forgettable first performer of *Not I* and the actress of Beckett's choice in later plays. Christina Tsingou continued to play Beckettian roles but in Greece she also directed his plays, very naturally starting off with *Endgame* in 1967 at the Thessaloniki State Theatre. When in 1973 she played Winnie in *Happy Days* at the Theatre 'Athina' it was under the direction of Roger Blin who had directed her, as Nell, in that first production of *Fin de partie* in London. These echoes alone would claim for the production a place in Beckett theatre history (though it was also admired for its set and costume designs by the leading Greek artist, Yiannis Tsarouchis).

The sense of being still so close to the start of it all, as also to Beckett, clearly made it more likely that such directors as Roger Blin and Tsingou would be careful in their handling of the texts. In contrast, Greek productions in more recent years have often been libertarian, with little or no sense of a need to keep close to Beckett's wishes. Another Greek actress/director, Roula Pateraki, led the way with a *Happy Days* in 1990 which offered two different versions of the play, neither following the lay-out of the original text. In one variation her Winnie was imprisoned not in the mound but by a spectacularly confining crinoline; in the other she sat in candlelight at a table, reading her part aloud, while Willie, at a piano, made his rare occasional responses in musical phrases. Edward Albee, a profound admirer of Beckett, and like him both playwright and director, was not impressed by the crinoline when it travelled as far as Los Angeles. It might be of course that the possibility of playing such tricks and attracting audiences with them is a testimony to the strong life in the plays, for productions in Greece continue to draw interest. *Rockaby* was the starting point for another actress/director, Anna Kokkinou, who presented that play at Sfenthoni Theatre in 1999, going on in 2003 to perform in *Happy Days* and construct an ambitious Beckett Festival of the shorter plays. In this powerfully female context it is only right to mention the attraction *Rockaby* also had for a male director, Theodorus Terzopoulos, well known for his experiments with Greek tragedy. He produced the play in 2002 and again, with others, in the following season. The attraction of the short later plays apparent in recent Greek experience has become increasingly common in many parts of the world.

Japan, also a country with an esteemed ancient drama, entered the Beckettian scene at a time when the Shingecki groups active there in the 1960s were leaning toward Stanislavski and naturalism. But they also supported experimental productions of plays from Europe in quite different styles, as in one early production of *Waiting for Godot* in 1965, directed by a woman, Hiroko Watanabe. Her aim, it seems, was to achieve a poetic simplicity with suggestions of Nō stylisation in such details as a notably abstract tree. A leading scholar, Yasunari Takahashi, was later to encourage interest in Beckett's art and instigate creative discussions in London, linked to performances by Nō actors. More recently, another ancient Japanese form of art has been brought into the Beckettian scene by Junko Matoba in her book *Beckett's Yohaku*. She traces fascinating comparisons between the 'white' undrawn space in Japanese monochrome painting and Beckett's handling of empty stage space in his later, shorter plays.[6] Japan showed that it could provide the talent required for silent acting in such a play as *Act Without Words 1* when it was performed in 1962 by Yoshi Oida, later to become a leading actor in Peter Brook's company. It was not, of course, all stylisation and poetic effect in the early reception of Beckett's plays in Japan. Other local traditions, notably a fondness for slapstick, also came into view, rather excessively according to some accounts. The very first production of *Godot* in Japan by the Bungakusa Theatre Company apparently laid considerable over-emphasis on the comic, vaudeville aspects of Beckett's theatrical art. However, comedy needed to have its place in Beckett's plays assured, perhaps especially in a theatre where stylisations such as those of Nō drama were still potent.

Commentators such as Mariko Hori Tanaka, on whose accounts I have drawn,[7] point to the more extreme freedoms that were taken as time went on. Some free-wheeling productions evidently provided little more than an unusual starting-off point for a more familiar local form of theatre; often broad melodrama or farce. Others, though keeping closer to the original, have still felt free, notably in the 1980s, to make quite drastic changes. Lines amounting to one-third of the dialogue have been cut in a production of *Godot* and the play has been performed with an all-female cast, an approach specifically outlawed by Beckett. Yet here again, as elsewhere, perhaps such responses can be seen as an indication of the power in the plays to attract a wish to be somehow involved in them.

Beckett's is a complex legacy, hard to define. It draws actors and audiences to it, as drama must, through the action. But there are puzzles in the action. Is the name Godot meant to bring God to mind? That has often been dismissed as a crude notion yet it won't go away, the sense of yearning for some mysterious apotheosis is so strong. Similarly, at the start of *Endgame*, Clov's 'toneless' meditation on the 'end' evokes a biblical line of mighty resonance: 'Finished, it's finished, nearly finished, it must be nearly finished.' The reach of imagination into these regions is an aspect of Beckett's poetic power which translation to another language need not obscure. It seems so, at least, from the success the plays continue to have all over the world.

What of the other aspect of poetic quality: the arrangement of well-chosen words in an evocative rhythm? Though much will be lost in translation much will remain, and of course, texts written, as Beckett's were, in two or even three major languages can travel widely in the world in their original form. No other modern playwright has with such seeming ease lifted the rhythms of colloquial speech, its common words and turns of phrase, into a poetry of the stage which co-exists with a comedy alert to many sorts of absurdity. One of his most fervent admirers among American playwrights, David Mamet, explaining to an interviewer why Beckett was to him 'a kind of a demigod', pushed away suggested reasons to do with 'themes', saying simply he admired him so much 'because the son of a gun could write'.[8] We know what he means by this whenever we hear the lines delivered on stage by actors who can bring out to the full, as Michael Gambon and the youthful comic Lee Evans did in a recent *Endgame* in London, the power of simple words to move from laconic repartee into spell-binding rhythms. The closing moments of *Godot* are pure poetry. When Estragon asks, 'Why don't we hang ourselves?', going on to untie the cord fastening his trousers which then fall down, we are close to music hall and at the same time in a dimension far beyond it. Comedy flickers again with Vladimir's practical 'We'll hang ourselves tomorrow,' but we are reminded by his next remark, 'Unless Godot comes,' of the great mystery keeping them there; the hope of salvation. Finally, the complex spiritual condition of scepticism, disappointment and persisting will to believe in Godot is gathered up for us into seven ordinary words (and a stage direction), now become infinitely poignant:

VLADIMIR: Well? Shall we go?
ESTRAGON: Yes, let's go.
[*They do not move*]

Beckett also seized on opportunities offered by radio, tape-recorders and so forth to convey on stage a sense of the sad poetry mixed with the ordinariness as well as the laughable absurdities of life. Through the mundane apparatus of the tape-recorder in *Krapp's Last Tape* he involves us in the complex being of the solitary man on stage, so like and yet unlike the confident younger self on tape. Beckett's fiction has made its way on to the stage partly, no doubt, because of the opportunities offered by the media to convey these variations of 'persona' within the limits of a single voice, an art finely demonstrated by David Warrilow and Barry McGovern among other actors.

What might not have been expected from a master of words was an equal mastery of the scenic image. Beckett's often extraordinary stage scenes are an important part of his legacy to the modern theatre, showing, as they do, how visual effects can reflect at a deep level poetic as well as theatrical force. One such effect is the quiet appearance of a leaf on the solitary tree in *Godot*. More fantastically, there is the distortion of ordinary features of a living room in *Endgame*; the windows so high that a ladder is needed to see out of them, the one door allowing no real exit, the two ashbins parked by Hamm's armchair (was Beckett joking when in his opening stage direction he described this set as a 'Bare interior'?). Yet realism remains; in dialogue, in character. This is true also of *Happy Days*, a play which strangely gains in realism and poignancy from the fantastic nature of the scenic image, the woman buried up to her waist, then neck, in a mound of earth. It reminds us of the end to which all must come, while allowing for some stage fun and a fine show of Winnie's brave humour.

In the later, briefer plays, scenic images of often terrifying power are created from empty stretches of a stage dark except for a light trained on some part of a human figure; the heads in urns of *Play*, the babbling Mouth in *Not I*. There is comedy here, especially in the jealous squabblings of *Play*. But these plays have to be brief: no audience could endure for long the tense scenic situations; the endless probing of the spotlight of

Play as it seeks for some 'truth'; the unyielding focus on Mouth, an illuminated facial feature isolated high above stage level, panting out a life story which she resists accepting as her own. In both plays the scenic image speaks silently of some other dimension where truth will at last be known. Religious implications cannot be ruled out, in this or indeed in any other of the plays.

Beckett kept a close watch on his plays in performance, and often directed them, following his production of *Endspiel* in 1967 with the Schiller Theater. Though protective of his plays' integrity, he was always ready to approve or admire when he saw something unorthodox that worked. There is encouragement here for changes of that sort in future productions, especially perhaps for adaptations of the fiction. The Irish director Robert McNamara, looking forward in the early nineties to big developments in this 'relatively uncharted' field, warned that such adaptations, whatever form they took, should conform to the 'voices' of Beckett's vision.[9] These warnings, which should surely apply equally to the plays, make production a testing enterprise but also one that will continue to attract original talents of many kinds and in many forms of theatre art.

Audiences in different parts of the world are no doubt waiting for such developments. There was a warm reception in 2004 for the production of *Godot* which the Dublin Gate Theatre took to China, playing at Shanghai and Beijing. In their programme for the forthcoming centenary several of the plays will be shown, both in Dublin at the Gate and in London at the Barbican, as in 1999. It is good also to know that the Royal Court Theatre, where so much began, has an exciting project in mind for the autumn of the centenary year: a production of *Krapp's Last Tape* with Krapp played by Harold Pinter, a great admirer and friend of Beckett. America will be marking the occasion, notably with an event in Florida under the aegis of Stan Gontarski. France plans a Beckett festival in

Aix-en-Provence and a large-scale celebration in Paris, including, possibly, a controversial *Happy Days* with a Willie absent from the scene. And in the autumn, at the Guildhall Theatre, the first director to present *Godot* in English to a public audience, Peter Hall, will be showing his much praised, latest production of the great play.

Right at the heart of Beckett's legacy is this power of the plays to make us look forward to such events when they live again in the theatre of the day. Beckett will be with us, a live force, in the productions and plans for what will surely be an unforgettable centenary.

NOTES

CHRISTOPHER MURRAY

introduction: panting on to a hundred

1 Samuel Beckett, *The Complete Dramatic Works* (London: Faber & Faber, 1990), pp. 191–2. Unless otherwise stated, all quotations from Beckett's plays refer to this edition, cited as *CDW*, from which page numbers will be cited in the text.

2 Ibid., p. 425.

3 Patrick Kavanagh, *Collected Pruse* (London: MacGibbon & Kee, 1967), p. 266.

4 Beckett in interview with Tom Driver (summer 1961), in *Samuel Beckett: The Critical Heritage*, ed. Lawrence Graver and Raymond Federman (London: Routledge & Kegan Paul, 1979), p. 221.

5 Samuel Beckett, *Watt* (London: Calder Publications, 1976), p. 46.

6 Samuel Beckett, 'The Essential and the Incidental', *The Bookman*, LXXXVI (1934), reprinted in *Sean O'Casey: A Collection of Critical Essays*, ed. Thomas Kilroy (Englewood Cliffs, N.J.: Prentice-Hall, 1975), pp. 167–8.

7 Sean O'Casey, 'Not Waiting for Godot', in *Blasts and Benedictions: Articles and Stories*, ed. Ronald Ayling (London: Macmillan; New York: St Martin's Press, 1967), p. 51.

8 Arthur Miller, *Collected Plays* (London: Cresset Press, 1958), p. 21. The earlier quotation is from p. 8.

9 Samuel Beckett, *Proust [and] Three Dialogues* (London: Calder and Boyars, 1965), p. 28.

10 Christopher Marlowe, *Doctor Faustus*, 1.3.76, in *The Complete Plays*, ed. J.B. Steane (Harmondsworth: Penguin, 1969), p. 275.

11 Beckett, *Proust*, p. 67.

[12] James Joyce, *A Portrait of the Artist as a Young Man* (Harmondsworth: Penguin, 1960), p. 204.

[13] Samuel Beckett, 'First Love', in *The Complete Short Prose*, ed. S.E. Gontarski (New York: Grove Press, 1995), pp. 25–6. The quotation which follows is from p. 26.

[14] Samuel Beckett, *Eleutheria*, trans. Barbara Wright (London: Faber & Faber, 1996), p. 136. Subsequent quotations are from this edition and will be referenced by page numbers.

[15] It has recently been argued that Beckett was indebted to Pirandello for this kind of metatheatre. See Chiara Lucarelli, 'Behind the Mask: Tracing Pirandello's Legacy in Irish Theatre', PhD Diss., UCD Dublin, 2005.

[16] Samuel Beckett, 'Three Dialogues', in *Disjecta: Miscellaneous Writings and a Dramatic Fragment*, ed. Ruby Cohn (London: Calder Publications, 1983), p. 145.

[17] Samuel Beckett, *Nohow On: Company, Ill Seen Ill Said, Worstword Ho* (London: Calder Publications, 1992), p. 101.

[18] Kavanagh, *Collected Pruse*, pp. 266–7.

TERENCE BROWN
Beckett and irish society

[1] Samuel Beckett, 'Homage to Jack B. Yeats', in *Disjecta: Miscellaneous Writings and a Dramatic Fragment*, ed. Ruby Cohn (London: Calder Publications, 1983), p.149.

[2] Brian Inglis, *West Briton* (London: Faber & Faber, 1962), p.13.

[3] J.V. Luce, 'Samuel Beckett's Undergraduate Course at Trinity College Dublin', *Hermathena*, 1171 (winter 2001), p.41.

[4] Anthony Cronin, *Samuel Beckett: The Last Modernist* (London: Harper Collins, 1996), p.14.

[5] Cited by Roger Little, 'Beckett's Mentor, Rudmose-Brown: Sketch for a Portrait', *Irish University Review*, 14.1 (spring 1984), p.39. I wish to express my indebtedness to this article.

[6] Samuel Beckett, *More Pricks Than Kicks* (London: Calder Publications, 1993), p.61.

[7] W.B. Yeats, *Autobiographies* (London: Macmillan, 1955), p. 559.

[8] Samuel Beckett, 'Recent Irish Poetry', in *Disjecta*, p.70.

[9] Samuel Beckett, *Murphy* (London: Pan, 1973), p.51.

[10] *Disjecta*, p.73.

[11] Cronin, *Samuel Beckett: The Last Modernist*, p.206.

[12] Samuel Beckett, *Watt* (London: John Calder, 1963), pp.168–9.

[13] Samuel Beckett, 'First Love', in *The Complete Short Prose, 1929–1989*, ed. S.E. Gontarski (New York: Grove Press, 1995), pp.33–4.

[14] Samuel Beckett, *The Complete Dramatic Works* (London: Faber & Faber, 1990), p.194.

[15] Samuel Beckett, 'The Calmative', in *The Complete Short Prose*, p.62.

[16] J.C.C. Mays, 'Young Beckett's Irish Roots', *Irish University Review*, 14.1 (spring 1984), 22.

GERRY DUKES
the godot phenomenon

All quotations from *Waiting for Godot* are taken from the text as printed in *The Complete Dramatic Works* by Samuel Beckett (London: Faber & Faber, 1990). Readers should be aware that the 1986 hardback issue of this book printed, in error, the 1956 text rather than the revised 1965 text.

[1] See Samuel Beckett, *En attendant Godot*, ed. Colin Duckworth (London: Harrap, 1966), p. xlviii, n. 1.

[2] Letter to Barney Rosset, Bird Special Collection Manuscripts (Grove Press Records, 1953–85, Syracuse University, 25 June 1953).

[3] Samuel Beckett, *Eleuthéria*, trans. Michael Brodsky (New York: Foxrock Inc., 1995). Also Samuel Beckett, *Eleutheria*, trans. Barbara Wright (London: Faber & Faber, 1996).

[4] Lawrence Harvey, *Samuel Beckett: Poet and Critic* (Princeton, N.J.: Princeton University Press, 1970).

[5] Éditions Privat (Paris, 1986).

[6] Samuel Beckett, *En attendant Godot* (Paris: Les Éditions de Minuit, 1952), 2005 reprint.

[7] The version quoted here is from Angela Moorjani's '*En attendant Godot* on Michel Polac's *Entreé des Auteurs*', in *Samuel Beckett Today/Aujourd'hui*, ed. by Marius Buning et al. (Amsterdam and Atlanta, GA: Rodopi, 1998). Another English version translated by Edith Fournier was published in *The New Yorker* (24 June and 1 July 1996).

[8] 'Texts for Nothing III' in Samuel Beckett, *Collected Shorter Prose 1945–1980* (London: Calder Publications, 1986), p. 80.

[9] See *No Author Better Served: The Correspondence of Samuel Beckett and Alan Schneider* ed. Maurice Harmon (Cambridge, MA: Harvard University Press, 1998), p. 24.

DECLAN KIBERD
murphy and the world of samuel beckett

[1] For a different version of this story, which carries the force of folklore, see John Calder, *The Philosophy of Samuel Beckett* (London: Calder Publications, 2001), p. 12.

[2] Samuel Beckett, *Murphy* (London: Pan Books, in association with Calder & Boyars, 1973), p. 36. Subsequent quotations from *Murphy* are from this edition, to which page numbers in parentheses refer.

[3] Hugh Kenner, *A Reader's Guide to Samuel Beckett* (London: Thames and Hudson, 1973), p. 134.

[4] Samuel Beckett, *The Complete Dramatic Works* (London: Faber & Faber, 1990), p. 38.

[5] James Joyce, *A Portrait of the Artist as a Young Man* (Harmondsworth: Penguin, 1960), p. 16.

[6] Eugene Webb, *Samuel Beckett: A Study of His Novels* (London: Peter Owen, 1970) p. 49.

[7] *Endgame,* in *The Complete Dramatic Works,* p. 101.

J.C.C. MAYS
beckett as poet: verse, poetry, prose poems

[1] Published by Calder Publications, London, 2002. Poems quoted and referred to below are to be found in this edition.

[2] The most helpful commentary on the poems themselves remains Lawrence E. Harvey's *Samuel Beckett: Poet and Critic* (Princeton, N.J.: Princeton University Press, 1970). Beckett's 1934 essay, 'Recent Irish Poetry' – collected in *Disjecta: Miscellaneous Writings and a Dramatic Fragment* ed. Ruby Cohn (London: Calder Publications, 1983), pp.70–6 – was unknown to Harvey and is important for the Irish context.

[3] For examples and discussion, see Michael Benedikt (ed.), *The Prose Poem: An International Anthology* (New York: Dell, 1976); Mary Ann Caws and Hermine Riffaterre (eds), *The Prose Poem in France: Theory and Practice* (New York: Columbia University Press, 1983); Stephen Fredman, *Poet's Prose: The Crisis in American Verse* (Cambridge: Cambridge University Press, 2nd ed. 1990); David Lehman (ed.) *Great American Prose Poems: From Poe to the Present* (Old Tappan, N.J.: Scribner, 2003).

[4] *From an Abandoned Work* in *Collected Shorter Prose, 1945–1980* (London: Calder Publications, 2nd ed. 1986), p. 131.

[5] In the version published by John Calder (London, 1978), pp. 45–6.

[6] In *The Beckett Trilogy: Molloy, Malone Dies, The Unnamable* (London: Pan Books, 1979), pp. 64–9.

[7] In *The Complete Dramatic Works* (London: Faber & Faber, 2nd ed. 1990), p. 58.

ANTHONY ROCHE

samuel beckett: the great plays after godot

[1] Samuel Beckett, *The Complete Dramatic Works* (London: Faber & Faber, 1990), p. 371. All future page references to Beckett's plays are to this edition and will be incorporated in the text.

[2] See, for example, Hugh Kenner, *Samuel Beckett: A Critical Study* (Berkley and London: University of California Press, 1961; rev. ed. 1968), p. 155: 'we fancy the stage, with its high peepholes, to be the inside of an immense skull.'

[3] For an evocative description of Patrick Magee, see Anthony Cronin, *Samuel Beckett: The Last Modernist* (London: HarperCollins, 1996), p. 470.

[4] Cited in James Knowlson, *Damned to Fame: The Life of Samuel Beckett* (London: Bloomsbury, 1996), p. 442.

[5] William Shakespeare, *Macbeth*, in *The Arden Shakespeare Complete Works*, ed. Richard Proudfoot, Ann Thompson and David Scott Kastan (Walton-on-Thames, Surrey: Thomas Nelson and Sons Ltd., 1998), p. 773.

ROSEMARY POUNTNEY

stringent demands: aspects of beckett in performance

[1] *Theatre Quarterly*, Vol. III, No. 2, London, 1973, p. 20.

[2] Reading University Library, MS. 1227/1/2/14.

[3] *Observer Review*, 2 May 1976, p. 36.

[4] Billie Whitelaw, *Who He?* (London: Hodder and Stoughton, 1995), p. 152.

[5] Preview in celebration of Beckett's seventieth birthday, 13 April 1976; director, Peter Hall.

[6] Royal Court Theatre, January 1973; director, Donald McWhinnie.

[7] For example *That Time* and *Rockaby*.

[8] Paris, October 1963; director, Roger Blin.

[9] Royal Court Theatre, January 1973.

[10] Letter to the author, 26 January 1973.

[11] March 1976; director, Francis Warner; lighting, David Colmer.

[12] Conversation with Samuel Beckett, Paris, March 1980.

[13] Ibid.

[14] Response to author's questionnaire, 1976.

[15] Conversation with Samuel Beckett, Paris, March 1980.

[16] Théâtre Jeune Publique, Strasbourg, April 1996.

[17] See James Knowlson and John Pilling, *Frescoes of the Skull* (London: Calder Publications, 1979), p.206.

[18] December 1995, organised by W.G. Sebald.

[19] Letter to Alan Schneider, Paris, 12 August 1957. (Quoted in *No Author Better Served: The Correspondence of Samuel Beckett and Alan Schneider* ed. Maurice Harmon (Cambridge, MA: Harvard University Press, 1998), p. 15.

[20] Samuel Beckett Archive, Reading University Library; see also *The Theatrical Notebooks of Samuel Beckett,* 4 Vols, eds. James Knowlson, *et al.* (London: Faber & Faber, 1992–1999).

[21] Garrick Theatre, London, 14–19 March 1994.

[22] Conversation with Jonathan Miller, Oxford, 22 June 2005.

[23] Conversation with Martin Esslin, Strasbourg, 4 April 1996.

[24] I am indebted to Martha Fehsenfeld for this information.

ANTHONY CRONIN
Beckett's trilogy

[1] Samuel Beckett, *The Unnamable*, in *The Beckett Trilogy: Molloy, Malone Dies, The Unnamable* (London: Pan Books, 1979), p. 288. Subsequent quotations are from this edition and will be referenced in the text by page numbers.

[2] In interview with Gabriel D'Aubarède (1961), in *Samuel Beckett: The Critical Heritage*, ed. Lawrence Graver and Raymond Federman (London: Routledge & Kegan Paul, 1979), p. 217.

DERMOT MORAN
Beckett and philosophy

[1] Samuel Beckett, *The Complete Dramatic Works* (London: Faber & Faber, 1990), pp. 64, 108, 94. All subsequent quotations from the plays refer to this edition, indicated by page numbers in the text.

[2] Samuel Beckett in his review of MacGreevy's *Jack B. Yeats: An Appreciation and an Intepretation* (1945), quoted in Gerry Dukes, *Samuel Beckett* (London: Penguin, 2001), p. 58.

[3] Tom Driver, 'Beckett at the Madeleine', Columbia Forum (Summer 1961), quoted in Martin Esslin (ed.), *Samuel Beckett: A Collection of Critical Essays* (Englewood Cliffs, N.J.: Prentice-Hall, 1965), p. 169.

[4] Samuel Beckett, *All That Fall*, in *The Complete Dramatic Works*, p. 191.

[5] See Deirdre Bair, *Samuel Beckett: A Biography* (London: Vintage, 1990), p. 310.

[6] Samuel Beckett, 'The Lost Ones', in *Collected Shorter Prose 1945–1980* (London: Calder Publications, 1984), pp. 159–78.

[7] Samuel Beckett, *All That Fall*, in *The Complete Dramatic Works*, p. 196.

[8] See Samuel Mintz, 'Beckett's *Murphy*: a "Cartesian Novel"', *Perspective* 2.3 (1959) and Hugh Kenner, 'The Cartesian Centaur', in Martin Esslin (ed.), *Samuel Beckett: A Collection of Critical Essays*, pp. 52–61.

[9] Samuel Beckett, *The Complete Dramatic Works*, p. 130.

[10] Samuel Beckett, 'Whoroscope', in *Poems 1930–1989* (London: Calder Publications, 2002), p. 6.

[11] See Rupert Wood, 'An Endgame of Aesthetics: Beckett as Essayist', in John Pilling (ed.), *The Cambridge Companion to Beckett* (Cambridge: Cambridge University Press, 1994), pp. 3–4.

[12] Deirdre Bair, *Samuel Beckett: A Biography*, p. 374.

[13] Samuel Beckett, *Murphy*, first appeared in English in 1938 (London: Calder Publications, 2003), p. 6.

[14] Samuel Beckett, *Endgame,* in Beckett, *The Complete Dramatic Works*, p. 126.

[15] Samuel Beckett, *Film* (London: Faber & Faber, 1972), p. 11.

[16] See Ruby Cohn, 'Philosophical Fragments in the Works of Samuel Beckett', in Martin Esslin (ed.), *Samuel Beckett: A Collection of Critical Essays*, pp. 169–77.

[17] Beckett, *Poems 1930–1989*, p. 9.

[18] Julia Kristeva, 'The Father, Love and Banishment', in *Desire in Language*, trans. Thomas Gora, Alice Jardine and Leon Roudiez (New York: Columbia U.P., 1986). Here Kristeva comments on Beckett's short story 'First Love' and on *Not I*.

[19] Alain Badiou, *On Beckett*, ed. Alberto Toscano and Nina Power (Manchester: Clinamen Press, 2004).

[20] G. Deleuze, 'The Exhausted' and 'The Greatest Irish Film' (Beckett's Film), in *Essays Critical and Clinical*, trans. Daniel W. Smith and Michael Greco (Minneapolis: U. of Minneapolis Press, 1997), pp. 152–74 and pp. 23–6.

21 See John Fletcher, 'Samuel Beckett and the Philosophers', *Comparative Literature* 17 (1965), and Richard Lane (ed.), *Beckett and Philosophy* (New York: Palgrave, 2002).

22 J.P. Sartre, *Politics and Literature* (London: Calder Publications, 1973), pp. 63–6.

23 T. Adorno, 'Trying to Understand *Endgame*', in Brian O'Connor (ed.), *The Adorno Reader* (Oxford: Blackwell, 2000), pp. 319–52.

24 Ibid., p. 322.

25 Ibid., p. 323.

26 See Derek Attridge, 'This Strange Institution Called Literature: An Interview with Jacques Derrida', in Jacques Derrida, *Acts of Literature*, ed. D. Attridge (London: Routledge, 1992), p. 60.

27 Richard Kearney, 'Beckett: The Demythologising Intellect', in Richard Kearney (ed.), *The Irish Mind* (Dublin: Wolfhound Press, 1985), pp. 267–93.

28 M. Blanchot, 'The Unnamable', in Lawrence Graves and Raymond Federman (eds.), *Samuel Beckett: The Critical Heritage* (London: Routledge & Kegan Paul, 1979), p. 120. See also M. Blanchot, 'Where Now? Who Now?', in Harold Bloom (ed.), *Samuel Beckett's Molloy, Malone Dies, The Unnamable*, Modern Critical Interpretations (New York: Chelsea House Publications, 1988), pp. 23–9, on *The Unnamable*, and his short obituary tribute, 'Oh All to End', trans. Leslie Hill, in *The Blanchot Reader*, ed. Michael Holland (Oxford: Blackwell, 1995), pp. 298–300.

29 Samuel Beckett, *Disjecta: Miscellaneous Writings and a Dramatic Fragment*, ed. Ruby Cohn (New York: Grove Press, 1984), pp. 171–3.

30 Wolfgang Iser, 'Subjectivity as the Autogenous Cancellation of Its Own Manifestations', in Harold Bloom (ed.), *Samuel Beckett's Molloy, Malone Dies, The Unnamable*, Modern Critical Interpretations, pp. 71–84.

31 Ibid., p. 74.

32 Eugene Ionesco, 'Dans les armes de la ville', (1957), quoted in M. Esslin, *The Theatre of the Absurd*, p. 23.

33 See John Calder, *The Philosophy of Samuel Beckett* (London: Calder Publications, 2001), pp. 62–74.

34 Beckett, *Endgame*, in *The Complete Dramatic Works*, p. 94.

35 Beckett, *Waiting for Godot*, in *The Complete Dramatic Works*, p. 46.

36 Günther Anders, 'Being Without Time: On Beckett's Play *Waiting for Godot*', in Martin Esslin (ed.), *Samuel Beckett: A Collection of Critical Essays*, p. 143.

37 See Martin Esslin, *The Theatre of the Absurd*, new edition (London: Methuen, 2001), pp. 19–20.

[38] John Calder, *The Philosophy of Samuel Beckett* (London: Calder Publications, 2001), p. 13.

[39] Beckett, *Endgame*, in *The Complete Dramatic Works*, p. 116.

[40] Samuel Beckett, *The Complete Dramatic Works*, p. 13.

[41] Beckett, *Waiting for Godot*, in *The Complete Dramatic Works*, p. 59.

[42] Beckett, *Malone Dies* (Harmondsworth: Penguin, 1965). First published in French as *Malone meurt* (1951), translated into English by the author and published by John Calder (1958).

[43] Ibid., pp. 100–101.

[44] Beckett, *Waiting for Godot*, in *The Complete Dramatic Works*, p. 15.

[45] Ibid., p. 58.

[46] Ibid., p. 60.

[47] Ibid., p. 59.

[48] Ibid., p. 39.

[49] Ibid., p. 42.

[50] Beckett, *Poems 1930–1989*, p. 115.

[51] Samuel Beckett, 'Texts for Nothing IV', in *Collected Shorter Prose 1945–1980*, p. 84.

RICHARD KEARNEY

imagination wanted: dead or alive

[1] Cited in Deirdre Bair, *Samuel Beckett: A Biography* (London: Pan, 1980), p. 417.

[2] Samuel Beckett, *Disjecta: Miscellaneous Writings and a Dramatic Fragment*, ed. Ruby Cohn (London: Calder Publications, 1983), p. 70.

[3] Samuel Beckett, *Proust [and] Three Dialogues: Samuel Beckett & Georges Duthuit* (London: Calder and Boyars, 1965), p. 20.

[4] Ibid., p.14.

[5] Ibid., p. 68.

[6] Ibid., p. 74.

[7] Samuel Beckett, *The Complete Short Prose, 1929–1989*, ed. S.E. Gontarski (New York: Grove Press, 1995), p. 154.

[8] Samuel Beckett, *The Beckett Trilogy: Molloy, Malone Dies, The Unnameable* (London: Pan, 1979), pp. 216–17. See also Richard Kearney, *The Wake of the Imagination* (London: Routledge, 1988), p. 308.

[9] *Disjecta*, p. 145.

[10] *Imagination Dead Imagine*, in *The Complete Short Prose, 1929–1989*, p. 184. Subsequent quotations are from this edition, to which page numbers given in parentheses will refer.

11 *The Portable Nietzsche*, ed. Walter Kaufmann (Harmondsworth: Penguin, 1976), pp. 95–6.

12 Beckett in interview with Tom Driver, in *Samuel Beckett: The Critical Heritage*, ed. Lawrence Graver and Raymond Federman (London: Routledge & Kegan Paul, 1979), p. 220.

13 Walter Benjamin, 'The Work of Art in the Age of Mechanical Reproduction', in *Illuminations*, trans. Harry Zohn, ed. Hannah Arendt (London: Fontana Press, 1992), p. 235.

14 Paul Ricoeur, *Temps et Récit* (Paris: Le Seuil, 1984), vol. 2, pp. 42–3.

15 *The Beckett Trilogy*, pp. 381–2.

JOHN BANVILLE
Beckett's last words

1 In *Collected Shorter Prose 1945–1980* (London: Calder Publications, 1984), p. 135.

2 Pierre Mélèese, *Samuel Beckett* (Paris: Seghers, 1966), quoted by Thomas Trezise, in *Into the Breach, Samuel Beckett and the Ends of Literature* (Princeton, N.J.: Princeton U.P., 1990), p. 3.

3 Quoted in Enoch Brater, *Why Beckett* (London: Thames & Hudson, 1989), p. 55.

4 In the trilogy of late works, *Nowhow On* (New York: Grove Press, 1996), p. 56.

5 Quoted in S.E. Gontarski, 'The Intent of Undoing in Samuel Beckett's Art', in *Modern Critical Views: Samuel Beckett*, ed. Harold Bloom (London: Chelsea House, 1985) p. 240.

6 *Proust [and] Three Dialogues with Georges Duthuit* (London: Calder and Boyars, 1965,) p. 103.

7 The trilogy *Molloy, Malone Dies* and *The Unnamable* (London: Calder and Boyars, 1959), p. 71.

8 Ibid., pp. 92 and 176.

9 Gontarski, in *Modern Critical Views: Samuel Beckett*.

10 Wolfgang Iser, 'The Pattern of Negativity in Beckett's Prose', in *Modern Critical Views: Samuel Beckett*.

11 *King Lear*, IV.i. 25–26.

12 *Nowhow On*, p. 116.

13 Quoted by Brater, *Why Beckett*, p. 7.

14 *Collected Shorter Prose*, pp. 133–4.

15 *Nowhow On*, p. 3.

16 Ibid., p. 46.

17 Ibid., pp. 67–8.

[18] Ibid., p. 86.

[19] Lawrence Graver, 'Homage to the Dark Lady', in *Women in Beckett*, ed. Linda Ben-Zvi, (Urbana and Chicago: University of Illinois Press, 1990), p. 148.

[20] *Nowhow On*, p. 53.

[21] Ibid., p. 89.

[22] Ibid., p. 113.

[23] Ibid., p. 99.

[24] Ibid., p. 69.

[25] Ibid., p. 84.

[26] *The Beckett Trilogy*, p. 191.

BARRY MCGOVERN
Beckett and the radio voice

[1] Samuel Beckett, *Company* (London: Calder Publications, 1980), p. 7.

[2] .Cited by Clas Zilliacus, *Beckett and Broadcasting: A Study of the Works of Samuel Beckett for and in Radio and Television* (Åbo: Åbo Akademi, 1976), p. 29.

[3] Samuel Beckett, *The Complete Dramatic Works* (London: Faber & Faber, 1990), p. 255. All subsequent quotations from the plays refer to this edition, and page numbers will be given in parentheses.

[4] Samuel Beckett, *The Complete Short Prose, 1929–1989*, ed. S.E. Gontarski (New York: Grove Press, 1995), p. 162.

[5] *The Beckett Trilogy: Molloy, Malone Dies, The Unnamable* (London: Caldar and Boyars, 1959), p. 309.

[6] Samuel Beckett, *Proust [and] Three Dialogues: Samuel Beckett & Georges Duthuit* (London: Calder and Boyars, 1965), p. 103.

[7] *The Beckett Trilogy*, p. 305; the preceding quotation is on p. 296.

[8] Cited by Katharine Worth, 'Beckett and the Radio Medium', in *British Radio Drama*, ed. John Drakakis (Cambridge: Cambridge University Press, 1981), p.197.

[9] *The Complete Dramatic Works*, p. 172. Subsequent quotations from *All That Fall* and Beckett's other radio plays are from this edition, to which page numbers refer.

[10] Alec Reid, *All I Can Manage, More Than I Could* (Dublin: Dolmen Press, 1968), p. 88.

[11] *The Beckett Trilogy*, p. 418.

[12] Ibid., p. 418.

[13] *The Complete Dramatic Works*, p. 297.

[14] In the original edition, in *Ends and Odds: Plays and Sketches* (London: Faber & Faber, 1977), p. 99, the word here is 'little'.

[15] Beckett to Barney Rosset, 27 August 1957, cited by Zilliacus, *Beckett and Broadcasting,* epigraph, n.p., emphasis in original.

[16] Samuel Beckett, *Stirrings Still,* in *The Complete Short Prose, 1929–1989,* p. 261.

[17] *The Beckett Trilogy,* p. 16.

KATHARINE WORTH
Beckett on the world stage

[1] Ann Beer, 'Beckett's Bilingualism', in John Pilling (ed.), *The Cambridge Companion to Beckett* (Cambridge: Cambridge University Press, 1994), p. 215.

[2] Ruby Cohn, *A Beckett Canon* (Ann Arbor: University of Michigan Press, 2001), p. 358.

[3] David Bradby, *Beckett: Waiting for Godot* (Cambridge: Cambridge University Press, 2001), p. 104.

[4] James Knowlson, *Damned to Fame: The Life of Samuel Beckett* (London: Bloomsbury, 1996), p. 421 (Beckett's letter to Barney Rossett, 17 January 1956).

[5] Billie Whitelaw, *Billie Whitelaw: Who He?* (London: Hodder and Stoughton, 1995).

[6] Junko Matoba, *Beckett's Yohaku* (Tokyo: Shinsui-sha, 2003).

[7] Unpublished account by Japanese scholar Mariko Hori Tanaka (following from earlier research for M.A. degree at Royal Holloway, University of London, in 1992).

[8] In Lois Oppenheim, *Directing Beckett* (Ann Arbor: University of Michigan Press, 1994), p. 289.

[9] Ibid. p. 227.

NOTES ON CONTRIBUTORS

CHRISTOPHER MURRAY is Associate Professor of Drama and Theatre History in the School of English and Drama, UCD Dublin. A former editor of *Irish University Review* (1986–97) and chair (2000–03) of the International Association for the Study of Irish Literatures (IASIL), he is author of *Twentieth-Century Irish Drama: Mirror up to Nation* (1997) and *Sean O'Casey Writer at Work: A Biography* (2004), and has edited *Brian Friel: Essays, Diaries, Interviews 1964–1999* (1999). He is currently preparing *Selected Plays of George Shiels* for Colin Smythe's series Irish Drama Selections.

TERENCE BROWN is Professor of Anglo-Irish Literature in Trinity College, Dublin. He is also a Senior Fellow of the college, a member of the Royal Irish Academy and of Academia Europaea. He has published extensively on Irish literature and cultural history and has lectured on those subjects in many parts of the world. The third edition of his *Ireland: A Social and Cultural History* was published in 2004.

GERRY DUKES lectures in literature at Mary Immaculate College, University of Limerick. His first substantial contact with Beckett's work came about with the actor Barry McGovern as they prepared the script for Barry's one-man Beckett show *I'll Go On* which opened at the Gate Theatre for the Theatre Festival in 1985 and subsequently toured to many venues around the world. Since then Gerry Dukes has written many articles and essays on aspects of Beckett's dramatic and prose writings. In 2000 Penguin published his annotated edition of Beckett's postwar novellas and in 2001 his *Illustrated Lives: Samuel Beckett* appeared from the same publisher. It is currently in print from Overlook Press in New York.

DECLAN KIBERD is Professor of Anglo-Irish Literature and Drama in the School of English and Drama, UCD Dublin. Among his books are *Inventing Ireland* (1995), *Irish Classics* (2001) and *The Irish Writer and the World* (2005). In addition, he wrote the commentary for the RTÉ television documentary on Beckett, *Silence to Silence* (1985).

J.C.C. MAYS retired as Professor of Modern English and American Literature at UCD in 2004. He is the author of several essays on Beckett, Hugh Kenner calling his selection for the *Field Day Anthology* (1991) 'the best short introduction to Beckett ever printed'. His most recent publication is an edition of Yeats's and Moore's collaborative play *Diarmuid and Grania* for the Cornell Yeats series in 2005.

ANTHONY ROCHE is a Senior Lecturer in Anglo-Irish Literature and Drama in the School of English and Drama at UCD Dublin. His publications include *Contemporary Irish Drama: From Beckett to McGuinness* (1994) and the forthcoming *Cambridge Companion to Brian Friel*. He is currently the Director of the Synge Summer School.

ROSEMARY POUNTNEY lectured at Jesus College, Oxford, from 1984 to 2002, during which time she performed in *Not I*, *Footfalls* and *Rockaby* in Europe and elsewhere. Her *Theatre of Shadows: Samuel Beckett's Drama 1956–1976* (1988) considers the plays from their genesis in manuscript to their performance on stage.

ANTHONY CRONIN is a poet, novelist, biographer and essayist. He is the author of ten books of verse, of which the most recent is his *Collected Poems* (2000). His biographies include *Samuel Beckett: The Last Modernist* (1996). In 1985 he received the Marten Toonder award for his contribution to Irish literature and was recently elected a Saoi of Aosdána.

DERMOT MORAN is Professor of Philosophy at UCD Dublin and a member of the Royal Irish Academy. He has previously taught at Queen's University Belfast and St Patrick's College, Maynooth, and has held visiting positions at Yale University, Connecticut College and Rice University. He has published widely on medieval philosophy and contemporary European philosophy. His books include *The Philosophy of John Scottus Eriugena* (1989; reissued 2004), *Introduction to Phenomenology* (2000) and *Edmund Husserl: Founder of Phenomenology* (2005).

RICHARD KEARNEY holds the Charles Seelig Chair of Philosophy at Boston College and is the author of many books on European philosophy and Irish culture. His most recent publications include a trilogy, *The God Who May Be* (2001), *On Stories* (2002) and *Strangers, Gods and Monsters* (2003), and *Debates in Continental Philosophy: Conversations with Contemporary Thinkers* (2004).

JOHN BANVILLE is a novelist, whose latest novel *The Sea* won the Man Booker prize for 2005. Gallery Press has recently published *Love in the Wars*, his version of Heinrich von Kleist's *Amphitryon*.

BARRY McGOVERN is an actor whose work has included a close association with the work of Samuel Beckett. He has played Vladimir in the Gate production of *Waiting for Godot*, directed by Walter Asmus, which has toured worldwide, as has his one-man Beckett show *I'll Go On*. His recording of the complete *Molloy, Malone Dies* and *The Unnamable*, produced by RTÉ and the Lannan Foundation, is now available on CD.

KATHARINE WORTH is Emeritus Professor of Drama and Theatre Studies and Honorary Fellow of Royal Holloway, University of London. Her many books on Irish and modern drama include *The Irish Drama of Europe from Yeats to Beckett* (1978), critical studies of Oscar Wilde (1983), Sheridan and Goldsmith (1992), and Beckett (1999, paperback 2001). In 1987 she adapted Beckett's *Company* for the stage, with Julian Curry in the solo role directed by Tim Pigott-Smith. In collaboration with David Clark, she also produced new versions of *Eh Joe* and of the radio plays *Words and Music*, *Embers* and *Cascando*, featuring Patrick Magee and David Warrilow, with new music composed by Humphrey Searle.